More Praise for
Be Yourself, Everyone Else Is Already Taken

"The title alone is such a profound reminder for all of us, and the book delivers a marvelous manual of authenticity. I'm so glad to recommend it and live its principles."

—SARK, author/artist, *Juicy Pens, Thirsty Paper*

"In this book Mike Robbins challenges us to be ourselves, speak our truth, and live with authenticity. Utilizing these principles will allow you to take your life, work, and relationships to the next level."

—Tom Rath, *New York Times* best-selling author, *StrengthsFinder 2.0*

"Mike Robbins has taken the concept of authenticity and put it on the map. With so many self-help books going over safe and well-worn territory, here is a groundbreaking and well-written treatise on something we all need and that has before this eluded clarity. This is an excellent book!"

—Fred Luskin, Ph.D., author, *Forgive for Good*, and director of the Stanford Forgiveness Project

"*Be Yourself, Everyone Else Is Already Taken* is a bold call for each of us to 'wake up' and be real. As Mike Robbins models, writes about, and teaches us, our world needs people who are willing and courageous enough to be vulnerable and authentic. This is an important book that gives you a pathway to being more real in your life, your work, and your relationships."

—Lynne Twist, author, *The Soul of Money*, and cofounder of The Pachamama Alliance

"We criticize politicians for not being real with us, but when is the last time you tried to distinguish between your own 'public self' and the real you? Mike Robbins has tackled this timely topic with great skill and depth. What does it mean to live authentically? Are you truly being yourself? The answers are all here in this highly accessible, eye-opening book that is certain to have an impact on your life."

—Susan Page, author, *Why Talking Is Not Enough*

"Mike Robbins knows the secret about the difference between presence and performance that all we perennial adolescents have to learn in this culture to finally grow up. And he is very articulate about it! He teaches that authenticity, intimacy, joy in living, and success in life depend upon our ability to be present to each other and honestly report what we have done, what we think, what we feel, and what we notice. And he also knows that we have to stick with each other until we are clear and complete, whether, in the end, we agree or disagree—no schemes, no hidden agendas, no bullshit. More power to you, Mike! This is a wonderful book!"

—Brad Blanton, Ph.D., author, *Radical Honesty*

"I cannot think of a better person than Mike Robbins to write a book on authenticity. He totally gets it and he knows how to communicate it. This is one of those books that will have you say, 'that book changed my life!'"

—Rich Fettke, coauthor, *Extreme Success*

"Mike Robbins is a model of everything he teaches. *Be Yourself, Everyone Else Is Already Taken* is a call to action. It challenges all of us to be who we are and to live authentic lives."

—Yvonne and Rich Dutra-St. John, coauthors, *Be the Hero You've Been Waiting For*, and cofounders of Challenge Day

"Mike Robbins and I were both blessed to have Richard Carlson as our dear friend. It's through Richard that I have come to know Mike, whom I have discovered to be one of the most kind, positive, and loving human beings I've ever had the privilege to know. He has discovered how to be himself, his true Self, and with great candor, humility, and eloquence shares with the reader how to achieve the same in their own lives. This work is simple, complete, and profound. I highly recommend it for anyone who is done trying to be someone who they are not and wants to just be themselves."

Joe Bailey, author, *Fearproof Your Life*

"*Be Yourself, Everyone Else Is Already Taken* is written with openness and passion. In this powerful book, Mike Robbins teaches us simple but profound ways to be more real and conscious in our lives and relationships."

—Kris Carlson, author, *Don't Sweat the Small Stuff for Women*

"Mike Robbins's wonderful new book, *Be Yourself, Everyone Else Is Already Taken*, is a brilliant, insightful guidebook on the path to freedom . . . freedom from the fear of being unacceptable and unworthy . . . freedom from the fear of not being 'enough.' Inside you—right now—a voice is crying out to be liberated from that prison of fear. Your heart longs to be free from pretense, deception, and insecurity. Your deepest, most 'authentic' being is crying out for honesty, acceptance, and unconditional love. Nurture that yearning and give that voice a song by reading and digesting this delicious, empowering book. I highly recommend it!"

—John Welshons, author, *Awakening from Grief*

"This book is for everyone who ever second-guessed themselves. Mike Robbins shows you how to face your fears and tell the world the truth about who you really are. An inspiring writer—and a really cool guy—Mike Robbins is like Wayne Dyer meets Tony Robbins meets your most supportive friend. With inspiration, hope, and humor he takes you by the hand and shows you how to become who you were always meant to be."

—Lisa Earle McLeod, syndicated columnist, author,
Finding Grace When You Can't Even Find Clean Underwear

"Mike Robbins writes with clarity and heart. *Be Yourself, Everyone Else Is Already Taken* gives you powerful tools and insights for living your life with greater depth, awareness, and authenticity."

—Christopher Andersonn, author,
Will You Still Love Me If I Don't Win?

"An inspirational, accessible, and very practical book on cultivating essential practices and principles for maintaining one's authenticity, self-respect, and self-trust, in order to be a consistent and original contributing force in one's family, community, and the world. Relevant for all ages and professions!"

—Angeles Arrien, Ph.D., author, *The Second Half of Life*

be yourself
*everyone else is
already taken*

be yourself

everyone else is

already taken

Transform Your Life with the Power of Authenticity

Mike Robbins

JOSSEY-BASS
A Wiley Imprint
www.josseybass.com

Published by Jossey-Bass
A Wiley Imprint
989 Market Street, San Francisco, CA 94103-1741—www.josseybass.com

Jossey-Bass books and products are available through most bookstores. To contact Jossey-Bass directly call our Customer Care Department within the U.S. at 800-956-7739, outside the U.S. at 317-572-3986, or fax 317-572-4002.

Jossey-Bass also publishes its books in a variety of electronic formats. Some content that appears in print may not be available in electronic books.

Library of Congress Cataloging-in-Publication Data
> Robbins, Mike, date.
> Be yourself, everyone else is already taken : transform your life with the power of authenticity/Mike Robbins.
>> p. cm.
> Includes bibliographical references.
> ISBN 978-0-470-39501-1 (cloth)
> 1. Self-acceptance. 2. Self-esteem. 3. Self-realization. 4. Honesty. I. Title.
> BF575.S37R63 2009
> 158.1—dc22   2008053149

Printed in the United States of America
FIRST EDITION
HB Printing 10 9 8 7 6 5 4 3

contents

For my beautiful and amazing girls,
Samantha and Annarose. Thank you both for
being exactly who you are, for teaching me so much,
and for reminding me about what truly matters in life.
I love you both very much and I'm so grateful to be your daddy!

acknowledgments

My heart is filled with gratitude, love, and appreciation as I reflect on all of the wonderful people who've supported me in the creation of this book, in my life, and with my work.

First and foremost, Michelle Benoit Robbins, thank you for being such an amazing woman, wife, and mother. I'm so grateful to be married to you, and I appreciate the way you love me, the way you take care of our girls and our family, and how you show up in life. Thank you for supporting me in writing this book while you were pregnant and chasing a toddler around—you're incredible! Samantha Benoit Robbins, thanks for being my "extra spicy girl" and for the way you express yourself so passionately. You are such a great teacher to me and mommy, and I love you very much. Annarose Benoit Robbins, thanks for coming into this world and bringing your peaceful, beautiful spirit into our family. You had a big influence on this book from your mommy's belly, and we're so grateful to be your parents.

Richard Carlson, I miss you, brother, and feel your loving presence around and within me all the time. I continue to be grateful for all the ways you did and still do teach and mentor me. Kris Carlson, thank you for your amazing support of me, our family, and my work. Your generosity is incredible, and I appreciate all that you did to support me in writing this book.

Chris Andersonn, thank you for all that you've done and still do to help me get in touch with who I really am. Rich Fettke, your generosity and mentorship allowed me to step onto this path of writing, and I'm eternally grateful to you for that and so much more. Rich and Yvonne Dutra-St. John, you both inspire me in how you live your lives; do your work; and love each other with such passion and authenticity.

Lois Robbins (mom) thanks for your enthusiasm, for always encouraging me for to go for it, and for your commitment to me and our family. Ed Robbins (dad), thank you for teaching me how to express myself with passion and heart, and for reminding me that people are always more important than things. Lori Robbins, I'm grateful to be your brother and appreciate your love and support. Rachel Cohen, thanks for being you, for teaching me so much, and for always being willing to tell the truth.

Susan Miller, you're a great assistant and a wonderful friend. Thank you for taking such good care of me and supporting our entire family. Tyson Wooters, what a gift you've been to my life and my business. Thanks for all that you've done to support me and my work. Linda Chester, I appreciate having you as my agent and how you've helped make my dream of being an author come true. Alan Rinzler, thanks for your editing, for being who you are, and for teaching me so much about myself and about writing. Jennifer Wenzel, I'm grateful to work with you and to have you as a friend. Thanks for your contribution to this book and your dedicated support.

Steve Farrell, thanks for your contribution to this book and for all the ways you've contributed to my life for so many years. I'm grateful for our connection and for all the ways you've inspired me to "step out" and be myself. Theo Androus, your friendship and support continue to bless my life. Thanks for challenging me, teaching me, and being the incredible man that you are. Jess Bart-Williams, I love how real you are and appreciate your honest feedback, support, and friendship. Arthur Bart-Williams, thanks for being who you are and for how you support me and our family. John Brautovich, I'm grateful for our friendship and love how you show up in my life.

Jerry Benoit and Chris Seger, I'm grateful to have you as in-laws and appreciate your generous support. Georgie Weston, Rosa Ibarro, Kerry McIlvenna-Davis, Pam Quinn, Galaxy Hasley, and Amy Brain, thank you for taking care of my girls and supporting our whole family while I was writing and with all my travel and work. I'm so grateful for each of you.

Johnny and Lara Fernandez, I appreciate who you are, how you live your lives, and how you support me, my work, and our family. Sean Flikke, you are one of a kind, my friend, and I'm grateful for your love, support, and friendship. Asa Siegel, I love you, brother, and I'm grateful for the longevity, depth, and mutual support of our friendship. Susan Ariel Rainbow Kennedy, thank you for your friendship and inspiration. Fred Luskin, I appreciate your support, guidance, and mentorship.

Clint Greenleef, Terces Englehart, David Fererra, Scott Halford, and Holly Stiel—thank you for your contributions to this book, your honesty, and your support of me and my work. I'm honored to have you as friends.

Debra Hunter, Paul Foster, Nana Twumasi, Mike Onorato, Tolu Babalola, Adam Levison, Libby Powell, Carrie Wright, Carol Hartland, Erin Beam, Joanne Farness, Sophia Ho, Keira Kordowski, Susan Geraghty, Dave Horne, and everyone else at Jossey-Bass and Wiley who has been involved with this book and working with me, thanks for your hard work, commitment, and support. It's an honor for me to be a part of your team.

To all of those I didn't mention specifically—friends, family members, clients, colleagues, coaches, mentors, speakers, authors, teachers, teams, organizations, and others who've supported me in writing this book, along my path, and in my life and work—thank you for encouraging me, challenging me, teaching me, being there for me, and helping bring out the best in me.

Finally, as a way of practicing what I preach, being vulnerable, and celebrating myself—I appreciate me. For having the courage to write this book; for balancing everything in my life to make it happen; for my commitment and dedication to my own growth and to being real; and for my vulnerability, heart, and passion—I acknowledge myself!

be yourself
everyone else is
already taken

introduction

We live in a culture that is starving for authenticity. We want our leaders, our co-workers, our family members, our friends, and everyone else we interact with to tell us the truth and to be themselves. Most important, we want to have the personal freedom and confidence to say, do, and be who we really are, without worrying so much about how we appear to others and what they will think or say about us.

Sadly, however, even though we may say we want to live in a way that is true to our deepest passions, beliefs, and desires, most of us don't. We've been taught by our parents, teachers, spouses, friends, co-workers, politicians, the media, and others that it's more important to be liked and to fit in than it is to be who we truly are. In addition, many of us assume that who we are is not good enough, and therefore we're constantly trying to fix ourselves or to act like others we think are better than us.

However, the message of this book is, as the famous nineteenth-century author and poet Oscar Wilde so brilliantly stated, "Be yourself, everyone else is already taken."

1

Our Resistance to Authenticity

How often do you not do or say something you really want to because you're worried about what others might think? For most of us, including me, this happens many times on a daily basis. It's not that we intend to lie or deceive people in some overt or malicious way (although sometimes we do); it's mainly that we've been trained to do and say what we think others want us to, or what we guess will be "appropriate" in any given situation. We basically don't believe we can truly be ourselves and still "make it" in life.

When it comes to being authentic, the bottom line for most people I know or work with, and for myself as well, is that we're scared. We don't want to deal with what we imagine to be the consequences of authenticity—people's judgments and reactions, our own fears and doubts, possible failure or rejection, and more—so we just shut up and try to fit in. In addition, being true to ourselves takes real courage, commitment, and awareness. We often aren't willing to do what it takes to live our lives, do our work, communicate with others, create relationships, and look deeply at ourselves with a real sense of authenticity and truth. And, even when we do, it can be such a vulnerable and scary experience for us, we're not sure if we've ultimately done more harm than good—to ourselves and others.

As I travel around the country and speak to groups of all kinds—at businesses, nonprofits, government agencies, universities, churches, schools, public seminars, bookstores, and elsewhere—the challenge and desire for authenticity resonate deeply with the people I talk to. Most of the clients I've worked with one-on-one as a coach over the years have also struggled with their desire to have a real sense of authenticity in their lives. This is the paradox of authenticity; we both seek it and fear it at the same time.

How This Book Works

Be Yourself, Everyone Else Is Already Taken is a book that shows you how to move through the fears and limitations that prevent you from living true to yourself and how to bring more authenticity into your life. This book is about noticing and taking responsibility for the societal forces, people around you, and personal beliefs that can stop you from being authentic, and, most important, how you can move beyond what holds you back and be even more real with yourself and others in your life.

The ideas, principles, exercises, and practices laid out in this book give you specific techniques that allow you to

- Confront and transform your fear
- Express yourself fully and with confidence
- Deal with conflicts directly and resolve them effectively
- Take risks and go for what you truly want

- Keep things in perspective and have more fun
- Trust, forgive, and celebrate yourself
- Have more freedom, peace, and confidence in your relationships, your work, and your life

Authenticity is a process. It's something that continues to evolve throughout our entire lives. We can't become "authentic" in the same way we can earn a degree or accomplish a financial goal. Authenticity—like love, health, courage, awareness, patience, and more—is an ideal we aspire to and is something we must practice in the moment-by-moment, day-by-day experiences of life. Our ability to be real can and will deepen as we move through our journey of life, if we're conscious about it. Becoming more of who we really are is a process that never ends. As the famous saying goes, "there is no way to peace, peace is the way." The same could be said about authenticity.

No book, workshop, teacher, or anything else can make you "authentic" in a quick and easy way. Authenticity has to come from deep within you. This book, however, will help you confront some of your own personal challenges with being honest and genuine, and presents many powerful principles that when integrated into your life on a regular basis can allow you to access a deeper place of truth within you. This book can be a catalyst for you to be yourself in a more real way—thus giving you the profound peace, freedom, power, liberation, joy, depth, and fulfillment that accompany authenticity.

Understanding Authenticity

Authenticity is often misunderstood and misinterpreted. While most of us understand what it means on the surface—to be "real"—there is a much deeper awareness we must have of ourselves and of life if we're going to be authentic in our work, our relationships, and how we live.

There are a few specific reasons why authenticity is misunderstood.

- First of all, it's unique and personal for each of us, which can make it difficult to define in a universal way.
- Second, what it means for us to be "authentic" changes throughout our lives as we grow and evolve.
- Third, due to the complex nature of real authenticity, many of us are not willing to take an honest look at ourselves, speak our truth, or live our lives in a way that is true. This resistance is based on a number of personal factors—fear of embarrassment, family programming, societal expectations, and more.

What Authenticity Is Not

There are a number of common misconceptions of what it actually means to be authentic. These misconceptions add to the confusion we have about authenticity and also make it that much more difficult for us to live authentic lives. Many of us think that in order to be authentic . . .

- I have to know exactly what I want to do with my life, where I'm going, and what's important to me at all times.

- I have to get in people's faces, tell them how I think and feel, and let them know what's on my mind no matter what.
- I have to be unique and creative.
- I have to possess some kind of special talent or skill.
- I have to be fearless and not care what others think about me.
- I have to be passionate and always take risks.
- I have to be a loner and someone who "marches to the beat of my own drum."
- I have to be "cool."
- I have to have had lots of dramatic obstacles in my life that I've dealt with and overcome.

Some of the items on this list can, in fact, be aspects of authenticity and important in our journey toward deeper realness. The way we often try to put these myths into action, however, are in the form of ego-based posturing or superficial behaviors that don't amount to real authenticity. Whenever we think we *have* to do or be any particular way, chances are we aren't being authentic. While there's nothing inherently wrong with anything on this list, authenticity is much deeper than this.

What Authenticity Really Is

If you look up the word *authenticity* on Dictionary.com, the description reads, "The quality of being authentic; genuineness." When you then go to the word *authentic*, there are a few variations:

- Not false or copied; genuine; real: *an authentic antique.*
- Having the origin supported by unquestionable evidence; authenticated; verified: *an authentic document of the Middle Ages; an authentic work of the old master.*
- Entitled to acceptance or belief because of agreement with known facts or experience; reliable; trustworthy: *an authentic report on poverty in Africa.*
- According to Law. Executed with all due formalities: an authentic deed.

While all of these definitions make sense and essentially reinforce our general understanding that authenticity means "realness" and "genuineness," for the purposes of this book and our inquiry into what authenticity *really* is and how it affects our work, our relationships, and our own personal journeys of life, I think it's important for us to take a deeper cut at it.

Fundamentally, authenticity is about you being you—fully. It's about being yourself—understanding, owning, acknowledging, appreciating, and expressing all of who you are— both the light and the dark. Being authentic is one of the most challenging yet important aspects of our growth as human beings. It involves being totally honest about ourselves and with others. When we're authentic, we're vulnerable, aware, open, curious, and truthful above all else. We're in touch with our thoughts and our feelings, our doubts and our fears, our dreams and our passions, and so much more. When we're authentic, we're also able to own up to it when we're being phony. In my experience, all of this is much easier said than done. It's one thing for me to teach people about authenticity—and another thing altogether for me to be authentic in my life, my work, and my relationships.

Although there are many things we can do and say that are authentic, and much of what we'll discuss throughout this book focuses on action, real authenticity is actually as much about being as it is about doing. When we're *being* authentic, the words we say, the choices we make, and the actions we take will likely and easily be in line and congruent with our true selves.

Personal authenticity is not about proving anything to anyone; it's about *being* ourselves from our core. What's true for us is true for us, and when we know it and feel it within us, it doesn't need to be defended—just owned and ultimately lived.

The Benefits of Being Authentic

When we tell the truth and live our lives in an authentic way the benefits are profound. Authenticity can allow us to disentangle ourselves from much of our own pain and suffering, which frees us up to say, do, be, experience, and go for the things we really want in life. Here are some of the many benefits of being authentic:

- Confidence in yourself and a willingness to pursue your passions
- Freedom from things that hold you back—worry, excuses, other people's opinions, manipulation, avoidance, and more
- Improved health, decreased stress, and increased energy

- Enhanced connection with yourself and others
- Peace of mind
- Self-acceptance, self-appreciation, and self-love
- Fun

These and so many other wonderful things become possible when we have the courage to tell the truth, be ourselves, and live with real authenticity.

My Personal Journey of Authenticity

Like most people, I struggle with my own sense of personal authenticity and question on a regular basis who I am, how I show up in life, and some of the things I do and say. I say this with a deep sense of compassion, truth, and appreciation for myself and for all of us as human beings. If we're really honest about it, most of us are full of it most of the time. This is, of course, my judgmental opinion, but as I engage with others, many of them admit to this themselves and resonate with it in a deep way.

As you know, being inauthentic can and does cause a lot of pain in our own lives and for those around us. But even more harmful, as I've learned many times personally, is when we're being inauthentic and we don't even realize it.

I've spent most of my life doing everything I can to look good, be liked, and do well—all in an attempt to impress others, have them approve of me, and hear them say nice things either to me or about me to others. Much of my own striving for success in school, in sports, and in business has been about proving that I'm a good person and worthy of people's attention and admiration. As I've come to learn, this ego-driven, people-pleasing process is not only insatiable, it's damaging to us and to those around us.

At the same time, I've always had an innate fascination with what's real—for me, for others, and in general. In other words, I've been interested in and passionate about authenticity for most of my life. I've always had a pretty good "B.S. meter" and have resonated with and been drawn to people and situations that felt genuine to me.

What Failure Did for Me

I spent much of my childhood focused on sports, baseball especially. I loved playing baseball and was good at it. I played all through school, got drafted by the New York Yankees out of high school, but chose not to sign with the Yankees and instead to play baseball at Stanford University. After my junior year at Stanford, I got drafted again, this time by the Kansas City Royals, and signed a pro contract. In my third season in the Royals organization, at the age of twenty-three while I was still in the minor leagues, my baseball career ended abruptly when I tore ligaments in my left elbow and blew out my pitching arm. As I wrote in my first book, Focus on the Good Stuff, as devastating as this career-ending injury was for me, it also was one of the greatest lessons of my life—as it taught me, in somewhat of a painful way, the importance of appreciating life and myself as things are happening, not after the fact.

My favorite day of every baseball season as a kid and even as I got older was the last day. Usually on the last day of the season, you'd lose. And while I wasn't a big fan of losing, especially as a way to end the season, there were two things I loved about this final game. First of all, with the season ending, the pressure was off, at least for the moment. It no longer mattered how I performed, my rank and status on the team, how well I pitched, and so on. I felt like I was off the "hot seat" and also that all of my teammates whom I competed with, compared myself to, and often felt jealous of throughout the season were now all in the same boat with me—we were on the same level. The end of the season was like the great equalizer, and I appreciated that.

The second and more important reason that I loved this final game was that often some of the other guys on the team, even the tough ones, would break down and cry. Although this wasn't something that happened very often (because we'd all been taught, directly or indirectly, at a very early age that "boys don't cry"), when it did happen, it felt real and I appreciated it. It also made me feel like I wasn't such a freak because I cried myself from time to time, and wanted to on a regular basis—although I'd done a good job training myself to keep my emotions bottled up so as to not get made fun of by my teammates or others.

Thinking Something Was Wrong with Me

I spent much of my childhood, adolescence, and early adulthood feeling like there was something really wrong with me, even though on the outside I seemed to have it all together—good grades, good looks, lots of friends, good at sports, and basically "happy" and "successful." I figured I was just too sensitive, too paranoid, too insecure, too emotional, or something else, because I always seemed to doubt myself, to feel like an outsider, and to think I didn't measure up to those around me—regardless of my external "success." I felt like I was "faking it" all the time. But whenever I would see someone cry, or any time someone did or said something that seemed real or vulnerable, it always made me feel more connected to them personally and more normal myself.

As I've moved along through my life and listened to the fears, doubts, and insecurities of thousands of people, I'm now convinced that we all have times in life, some more than others, when we think something's wrong with us. There was and is nothing wrong with me for thinking and feeling this way, although I thought there was when I was younger and still sometimes go there when I'm feeling insecure these days.

I've also had many experiences that have taught me a great deal about myself and have brought me face to face with some of my deepest fears, blocks, blind spots, and places where I'm not being or living true to myself at all. As challenging and painful as some of these experiences have been for me, they've also been some of my best teachers, especially as it relates to being real.

Painful Losses

Over the past seven or eight years, I've experienced a number of painful losses, most significantly the death of my father in 2001 and the death of my friend and mentor Richard Carlson, author of *Don't Sweat the Small Stuff*, in 2006. These were two of the most important men in my life. In each case, their passing was unexpected, shocking, and incredibly painful for me. I had dealt with the death of people close to me before, but after both my dad and Richard died, the level of grief I felt when they each passed away was more intense than I'd ever experienced. In both cases, I was rocked to my core and wasn't sure how I would be able to move forward in my life without these two significant and special men. At the same time, these experiences were transformational.

There can be real magic in death. Ironically, it can wake us up to the gift of life, which is what my dad's and Richard's deaths both did for me in so many ways. They also scared me, saddened me deeply, and had me consider many things I never had before—both light and dark. In the days and weeks that followed their deaths, I felt intensely aware, present, alive, and authentic, which I greatly appreciated.

This is often the case when something like this happens and can be one of the beautiful blessings of a tragedy, even in the midst of the pain. Think of the times in your own life when something intense has happened, such as the death of someone close, getting laid off, divorce, a health scare, a major financial challenge, or something else that really gets your attention and wakes you up. Don't you often stop and appreciate life in a deeper way and interact with yourself and others from a more authentic perspective?

This can also be true for positive, "peak experiences" we may have—marriage, the accomplishment of a big goal, the birth of a child, a major milestone, and so on. Sadly, soon after these types of experiences we often lose our expanded perspective and awareness and go back to "life as usual." It's like a beautiful window of vulnerability and awareness opens up briefly and then closes quickly—we go back to being inauthentic and allow the busyness of day-to-day life to take over again. Even though I'm intensely aware of this phenomenon, I see it happen in my own life and around me all the time—and it always makes me sad.

The Freedom of Authenticity

This book is about retaining in everyday life the same level of conscious awareness we have after a tragedy, wake-up call, or peak experience. What if we could live in that heightened state of appreciation and authenticity on a more regular basis? Because this awareness comes from within us and is created by us, not by the external circumstances, we each have the power to live this way all the time if we choose to do so. It's not easy, takes a great deal of courage, and is often not encouraged or celebrated, but truly being ourselves and living our lives in this authentic way can give us real peace, passion, and purpose in life.

I've experienced, in my own life and in the lives of so many others, the power and freedom created by authenticity—an insight, a bold action, a difficult but important conversation, an apology, a raw expression of emotion, or a vulnerable admission. The times in my life when I've had the courage to do, say, or feel what was true for me at the deepest level, even though I've often been terrified, have been some of the most fulfilling, liberating, and exciting experiences I've ever had. As Eckhart Tolle says in his book *A New Earth*, "Only the truth of who you are, if realized, will set you free."

How to Use This Book

Be Yourself, Everyone Else Is Already Taken is separated into three sections. Part One, which includes two chapters, looks at why it can be hard for us to be authentic—the familial, cultural, and personal influences, thoughts, and fears that make it difficult for us to do and say what is true for us, or lead us to believe that who were are is not acceptable enough.

Chapter One focuses on the cultural and environmental factors, while Chapter Two looks at the more personal, psychological issues that stop us from being, doing, and saying what is true. For us to become more real in our lives, we have to first become aware of and take full responsibility for how we've internalized these external messages and also our own personal blocks that prevent us from being our true selves. Although this is a life-long, ongoing process of awareness, delving into these challenges here with a sense of realness, ownership, and compassion will allow you to take an honest look at where you are and what specifically makes it challenging for you to be authentic in your life, with your work, and in your relationships.

In both chapters of Part One, I share some examples from our society, from the lives of others, and from my own life personally that illustrate how and why authenticity can be challenging and what the ultimate impact of being inauthentic can be. I invite you to pay attention to the messages you've received and continue to receive, and also challenge you to take inventory of your own life and to assess honestly your own ability to be real. This first section of the book is vital in giving you the awareness, insight, and inspiration to become more of who you really are—by noticing and owning, with a sense of humor, awareness, and compassion, how full of it you can be and why. You have to shed some light into the darkness if you want to see where you're going and get beyond some of the places where you get stuck.

Part Two lays out the five principles of authenticity that I've developed over the past ten years working with individuals and groups as a speaker, seminar and workshop leader, and personal coach. They're each designed to empower you with new ideas, perspectives, and tips that lead to greater authenticity in your life and relationships—which thus creates more freedom, peace, and fulfillment for you and those around you. These five principles of authenticity are

> Principle 1:   Know Yourself
> Principle 2:   Transform Your Fear
> Principle 3:   Express Yourself
> Principle 4:   Be Bold
> Principle 5:   Celebrate Who You Are

These five principles are all powerful concepts that I teach people in coaching sessions, as well as in my seminars, workshops, and keynote speeches. Each principle builds on the one before it, leading you through a process that is designed to be enlightening, challenging, and empowering.

These principles, while simple to understand on the surface, take real courage to integrate into your life and relationships on a regular basis. Putting them into practice, however, will have a remarkable impact on you, on those around you, and on your level of genuine success and fulfillment in life.

Part Three is all about action. Making lasting change in our lives is not so much about what we know, but what we do. This final section of the book allows you to integrate what you've read and learned and come up with specific ways to put it into action in your life.

Interactive Exercises and Practices

Within most of the chapters there are interactive exercises for you to perform as you go along. Each exercise is designed to be done in the moment, as you read it. The exercises allow you to engage with the material in a personal and specific way that is unique to you and your life.

At the end of each chapter in Part Two there are several "practices" listed and described. Each suggested practice is usable, practical, and detailed. These are designed to have you actually *practice* the lessons of each principle of authenticity in your real life and relationships.

I've listed these practices to give you options and to spark your own unique thoughts. You're welcome to use them all, but the best approach is to pick one or two that either resonate with you deeply or scare you intensely (usually both signs of something important for you to pay attention to and do) and start using them in your life as you're reading the book. I also suggest that you talk about the exercises, the practices, and the book in general with other people in your life—this will make it be more relevant and give you the greatest impact from the material.

All of these exercises and practices are ones I use myself and also with my clients. They're "road tested" and designed to raise your awareness and to enhance your ability to be real, speak your truth, connect with others in an honest and vulnerable way, go for what you really want, and more.

Some of these exercises and practices are focused on you as an individual, and you can do them all by yourself. Others are designed to be done with a partner (husband, wife, friend, family member, co-worker, significant other, and so on) or with a group (work team, sports team, family, community group, and so on). It's a good idea for you to have a journal or notebook handy as you read through the book so that you'll have an organized place to write, make lists, and fully engage in these exercises and practices. Have fun with them and remember, they're just "practices," so you can't mess them up.

An Important Message from Me to You

Mother Teresa said, "Honesty and transparency make you vulnerable. Be honest and transparent anyway."

With these great words of wisdom in mind and as a context for this entire book, I want you to know from a deep place of authenticity and vulnerability within me that I am honored, excited, and scared as we embark on the journey of this book together.

I'm honored that you picked up a copy of this book and trust me to engage with you in this deeply personal inquiry of authenticity. I'm excited because I know how important this is and how liberating it can be for us and those around us when we have the courage to be ourselves, speak our truth, and go for what we want in life—even though it can be challenging.

And I'm scared because the little critical voice in my head, the "Gremlin" (which we'll talk about more throughout the book), keeps saying things to me like, "Who do you think you are talking to people about being real when you're so full of it yourself?" or "You don't have the guts to really say what you want to say in this book," or "None of this stuff is original—people either already know it or you're just ripping it off from someone else anyway." I share these doubts with you as a way of being transparent, practicing what I teach, and acknowledging my fear and going for it anyway.

This also leads me to an important note of caution to you—authenticity can be a bit tricky, difficult, and scary for most of us. We've each learned many creative ways to not tell the whole truth to ourselves and others, to pretend to be certain ways we think we're "supposed" to be, and to live our lives in a way that we hope helps us "make it"—none of which are usually all that authentic. It takes courage to live, work, and create relationships with a real sense of honesty and genuineness. For these and other reasons, this book may at times be challenging or confrontational for you to read, engage with, and integrate into your life—just as it was at many times for me to write. The concepts may be simple to understand intellectually, but to integrate these ideas into your life emotionally and to practice them on a regular basis with yourself, in your work, and in your relationships will take some real commitment, courage, and awareness.

I don't say this to be overly dramatic, confrontational, or self-righteous (all of which, however, are things I can be at times). This is not a "lite" discussion we're having here, and it is not theoretical. This is about your life, about your truth, and about you being real—it's not for the faint of heart, and in order to get any real value out of this book you must be willing to truly engage and do the work in your life.

Living with real authenticity, while incredibly liberating, is not something that comes easily to most of us, myself included. I acknowledge you for picking up this book, for your interest in living a genuine life, and for your willingness to learn, grow, and step outside of your comfort zone. Thanks for choosing to come along on this exciting, challenging, and liberating ride. Here we go. . . .

part one

∞

why it can
be hard to be
authentic

1

don't step out
of line

"You were born an original, don't die a copy."

—John Mason

Why is it hard to be authentic? More important, why is it hard for you to be authentic? This isn't an accusation or a judgment, it's an important question. If you can ask and answer this question honestly, without judging yourself (remember, it's hard for most of us), you're well on your way to becoming more of who you really are and ultimately more authentic.

Are we born inauthentic? No, I don't think so! So how did this difficulty in being authentic come to pass?

Understanding how we got to be inauthentic is not only more complicated to answer, it's essential for us to inquire into on our journey of authenticity. While I don't believe we're victims of our circumstances, nevertheless we're influenced by the culture in which we live; the people around us; and our own internal make-up.

This first section of the book focuses on why it can be difficult for us to be authentic and on some of the societal, familial, and personal influences—thoughts, feelings, attitude, beliefs, decisions, and choices—that can make authenticity so challenging for us. Each of us is unique and therefore has a separate set of influences and challenges, but many of these factors are also universal. Chapter One focuses on the cultural level, while the second chapter delves into things on a more personal and psychological level.

We Aren't Taught or Encouraged to Be Authentic

From the moment we come into the world, we immediately begin getting "trained." The doctors, midwives, nurses, parents, family members, and others we meet on our very first day of life begin taking care of us and at the same time imposing on us their rules, procedures, opinions, beliefs, and ideas of how the world works and how things should be. As the father of two very young girls (our older daughter, Samantha, is three and our baby girl, Annarose, is not even one yet), I'm well aware of this process and understand how necessary it is. If we don't take care of our babies for many years after they're born, they could not and would not survive. This human dilemma, however, highlights one of the core conflicts we all face—how do we know what it means to be who *we* truly are when how we learn about life is through the filtered perspectives of the people who raise us and the culture in which we live?

In addition, the survival training we get as young children and throughout our lives is often at odds with our desire and ability to be authentic. Directly and indirectly we're taught not to "step out of line," literally and figuratively. There are many factors and social institutions within our culture that either initiate or perpetuate this. Some do both. Let's take a look at some of the most significant examples of these influences and how and why they get in the way of our knowing and being who we truly are.

Family

Whether we come from families we consider "healthy" or those we consider "dysfunctional," most of us didn't learn to be authentic in our families. In fact, in most cases we learned the exact opposite. Why is this? Because most of the people in our families have a hard time being authentic, just like most of the people on the planet (you'll see that this is a theme throughout this chapter, section, and the book, by the way). In addition, most families—even "healthy" ones—have a lot of unresolved issues, conflicts, and unexpressed emotions that have an impact on each person within the family individually and the family unit collectively. This causes us to create certain dynamics in our families in which each of us plays a specific role based on years of unconscious thoughts, feelings, and behavior. These roles often create a lot of pain and frustration for us and others in our families, and they're not at all conducive to us being who we really are.

CHECK THIS OUT
Statistics About American Families

- According to the 2000 U.S. Census, more than 60 percent of all American children are from divorced families.
- According to the American Medical Association, 72 percent of American homes harbor someone with an addiction.
- According to a 2006 Harris Poll, approximately 33 million, or 15 percent, of all U.S. adults admit that they were a victim of domestic violence. Furthermore, six in ten adults claim that they know someone personally who has experienced domestic violence.

Many of the major life decisions we make—where we live; our career choices; what religion or spiritual path, if any, we choose to follow; whom to be in romantic relationships with and ultimately marry; if we have children and how many; what we spend our money on; whom we vote for in elections; how we take care of ourselves; and much more—are significantly influenced by our family members, regardless of how old we are, whether we're in regular communication with them, how far away they might live from us, and even in some cases whether or not they're still alive.

Many people follow in lockstep with the values or beliefs of their families, while others, especially in the past fifty years in our Western culture, have rejected the beliefs of their families and make it a point to let everyone know they are "doing it their own way."

Regardless of which end of this spectrum we find ourselves on, it's obvious that our families play a huge role in our ability or inability to be authentic. Most of us unconsciously run the decisions we make through this base-level filter and ask ourselves, "What will my family think? Given that we all needed the love, approval, and acceptance of our families for our survival when we were children and adolescents, many of us still operate as if that is the case today, when usually it's not. Others of us may have rejected this need years ago and operate in continuing opposition to our subjective recollection of our family's values and opinions.

Many of us, as we grow and evolve, learn to disentangle ourselves from our family of origin (parents, siblings, and so on) but then re-entangle with our spouses and our own children. It's the same phenomenon, just different players. In either case, when we do this (which most of us do, without even knowing it) we're not fully thinking and feeling for ourselves and we're letting the real or perceived expectations of others dictate who we are, what we can do, and how we think we're "supposed" to be.

I still find myself doing this all the time. As I sit here and write this book, I notice that my automatic filter of what I think I can and can't say is heightened, especially as it relates to my family. Wondering about what my mom, my sisters, my wife, my aunts and uncles, my in-laws, my daughters (when they're old enough), and others will think of what I'm writing influences what I'm willing to say.

Being aware of this is the first step in taking back our power and being more of who we are. Our family is the first and often most powerful force in our lives that we allow to take away our authentic voice and our real power. In most cases we were and still are given direct and indirect messages from our family to not be who we really are, but to be who and what they want us to be or think we should be or, at the very least, to not be who or what they would be embarrassed for us to be.

School

I wore a maroon polyester leisure suit with tan desert boots and a grey clip-on tie to my first day of kindergarten. Yes, my mother did actually love and care about me. She swears to this day that I insisted on that outfit myself—although I'm sure she got a real kick out of it. It was the late 70s, my older sister Lori was into the Bee Gees, Shaun Cassidy, and disco, so I guess I just picked up this odd fashion idea from some of that influence. I'm not really sure if this was an act of me being myself or not, but it definitely was unique, and the snapshots from that day are pretty funny. However, I learned something on that first day of kindergarten when the other kids laughed and I felt stupid that stuck with me for a long time and still lingers today: *Do everything you can to avoid being made fun of!*

I think most of us learn this lesson at some point early in our lives, especially at school. Education is so important, and most of us in this culture are fortunate to have access to it and for free. Sadly, however, we all have experiences in school with the other kids, as well as with many of the adults, that affect us in a negative way both mentally and emotionally. Our educational system often misses the boat big time when it comes our mental and emotional development, to say nothing of the quality of education itself.

I believe that most teachers, like most parents, have the best of intentions. But because most of the people involved in the school communities have a hard time being authentic themselves (like most people alive), just by watching the adults and the other kids around us on a daily basis, we often literally were "trained" to be inauthentic in school.

While things do seem to be getting better, and there is much greater awareness these days about important stuff like room setup, exercise, diet and nutrition, mental and emotional well-being, creativity, multiple learning styles, and more, most of us who are adults today grew up going to schools and sitting in classrooms where we were stuck in rows and forced to memorize lots of information simply because that was the way it had always been done and because the standards, test scores, and funding for the schools often depended on the enforcement of these things. Sadly, this is still the case in many schools today.

While there is clearly an important place for discipline, training, rules, safety, and much more—both at home and at school—much of the fear-based, ego-driven way in which we were taught in school did not encourage us to think for ourselves, allow us to express our real emotions, or give us the necessary tools to figure out who we are, what we want, and what's important to us.

Some argue that school was not designed for this in the first place and that much of the social and emotional training we need should come from home. However, given the amount of time we all spent in school, the relative dysfunction of many of our families, and the increased financial pressure placed on modern families to work more hours and leave their kids with others, school has become even more influential over the years in terms of the mental and emotional development of children and teenagers.

On average most of us spend fifteen years in school from the time we go to preschool at the age of three until the time we graduate from high school at the age of eighteen. Assuming we go on average of 180 days per year, for six hours each day, that's over sixteen thousand hours of school, or just about two full years of our lives, by the time we graduate from high school—without even factoring in our time in college or graduate school. Suffice to say, we spend a good amount of time in our formative years in school.

Regardless of our current age or where we grew up, most of us learned a great deal in school—both good and bad, as well as in and outside of the classroom. And, since the educational system is often devoid of many effective tools for how to really think, feel, express ourselves, and deal with the reality of life, most of us were trained to simply follow rules and retain information, and were given a long list of social norms we either follow or rebuke as we move through life.

I'm not an expert on education, and I realize that the opportunities and challenges within different schools and communities vary a great deal, but from my own experience growing up, going to school as a child, and even as I got older and attended a well-respected university (Stanford), I feel that there's not a lot we learn in school that teaches us about how to be ourselves, to speak our truth with confidence, and to live life in an authentic way.

Organized Religion

Organized religion is another powerful force and institution in our culture that can have a negative impact on our ability to be ourselves. This one is a little tricky for me to talk and write about, because I don't want to offend anyone. We all have our own personal opinions about religion and our own personal beliefs about the role of God or religion in our lives, and for most of us these opinions and beliefs are held sacred. Even if you're someone who doesn't believe in God; doesn't belong to an organized religion; and has never even gone to a church, synagogue, mosque, or spiritual gathering of any kind, you can still be mightily influenced by organized religion in our culture.

I have great appreciation and respect for everyone's spiritual path, and I even respect those who choose not to acknowledge one or don't think that God exists. I truly believe that "all paths lead to God." But, paradoxically, I think organized religion is an institution that can and does damage people deeply, especially as it relates to authenticity.

I heard Dr. Wayne Dyer a few years ago say, "That which is of God unifies us and that which is of the ego divides us. Therefore, in most cases organized religion, which divides much of the world and has for generations, is of the ego, not of God." When I heard him say this, I was shocked. I remember looking around to see if anyone else was as shocked as I was. There didn't seem to be that much reaction from the people around me. I then turned to my wife Michelle and said, "Wow, I can't believe he said that— he might get in trouble." Even though I actually agreed with what he said, my knee-jerk reaction was based on years of programming, and I immediately thought to myself, "That's blasphemy." Wayne Dyer, who is one of the most prominent spiritual teachers of our time and one of my personal favorites, spoke a deep truth that resonated within me. But on the basis of my own notions of what's "acceptable" to say about religion I was taken aback.

Religion can be a beautiful expression of spirituality, community, love, and service. So many good things are done by faith-based groups in our culture and throughout the world. But at the same time, I think religious doctrine, structure, and dogma in many cases stifle our creativity, our expression, and ultimately our authenticity. There are so many sad and painful stories of people being abused in very harmful ways by members of their religious community— leaders and others. And I've heard literally thousands of less dramatic stories from family members, friends, and clients over the years about how much fear, shame, and guilt they felt growing up based on what they learned or heard at church or temple.

I grew up quite confused in relation to religion and spirituality. My dad was raised Jewish and my mom Catholic, although neither of them really practiced their religions and we did not go to church or synagogue on any regular basis for the first few years of my life. A couple of years after my folks split up, when I was about five, my mom took my older sister Lori and me to St. Paul's Lutheran Church in our neighborhood because they had free meals on Wednesday nights and programs for kids, and it gave my single mom an opportunity to connect with other adults. I got baptized at age seven (so we could become official members of the church) and then as a teenager went through confirmation class and ultimately got "confirmed" as a Lutheran.

I didn't feel any real personal connection to God, Jesus, or the whole church experience as a kid or teenager. I wanted to, but it all seemed stuffy, outdated, and weird to me. I couldn't understand how or why it had anything to do with me, my life, or life in general. A pivotal moment for me in my relationship to organized religion happened in one of our confirmation classes. I raised my hand and asked Pastor

Merkel, our minister and teacher, "How can I be sure that Lutheranism is the 'right' religion? I want to make sure if I'm going to pick one, I pick the 'right' one. And, since I know other people who are from other religions, like my dad who is Jewish, does this mean that they are 'wrong'?"

Pastor Merkel was in his early thirties and in his first few years at our church. He was a bit stunned by this question from a somewhat self-righteous thirteen-year old who didn't really want to be in his confirmation class to begin with. I don't exactly remember what he said, and in hindsight I feel a little bad that I put the poor guy on the spot like that. I'm sure he did his best to answer my question and probably talked about the importance of faith, but whatever he said didn't satisfy me. I came to the conclusion that if there really was a God, He, She, or It probably wasn't looking down from above at all of us on earth and laughing at the vast majority of people who had picked the "wrong" version of organized religion.

The ideals and intentions of most organized religions—Divine teaching and practice—are beautiful, wonderful, and important in life. Sadly, however, the way that many of us, like me, experience organized religion and the influence that it has had on our society has not been all that supportive or empowering in our desire to be ourselves and live with authenticity.

Politics

The 1939 movie Mr. Smith Goes to Washington depicts a young, naïve "do-gooder," played by Jimmy Stewart, who gets appointed by the crooked political machine of his state to become a United States senator for the final few months of the term of their recently deceased elected senator. The powers that be figure that this young kid is smart enough to do the job, but clueless enough to not ask any questions or get in the way of their agenda. The movie goes on to point out how corrupt and cynical the politicians and media in Washington are, and in the end the honest, high-minded Smith prevails in a perfect Hollywood/Jimmy Stewart/Frank Capra (the writer and director of this film, along with It's a Wonderful Life and many others with similar themes) kind of way.

This is one of my favorite movies, and every time I watch it I'm amazed by how much has remained the same in terms of the opinion we hold and the reality of how political leaders operate in Washington and in general.

Unfortunately, politics is another institution that reinforces and exemplifies inauthentic behavior. We're all very aware of the lying, cheating, and hypocrisy that take place in politics today, and with the twenty-four-hour cable news cycle we see it and hear it all day and all night. Even with this increased scrutiny and pressure, most politicians still look us in the eye and lie to us on a regular basis. Whether it was President Nixon saying, "I am not a crook," President Clinton saying, "I did not have sexual relations with that woman, Ms. Lewinsky," or President Bush saying, "Iraq has stockpiles of weapons of mass destruction," we get lied to by politicians in big ways and small ways all the time.

While most people don't want or expect bald-faced lies from their political leaders, at least not the ones they respect and support, we assume that they'll pretty much do and say whatever they need to in order to get elected and have high approval ratings. The post-debate gathering place for the media and the people who work for politicians running for president is called the "spin room." I don't know what's worse; that it has that name or that we aren't more upset or concerned about it.

CHECK THIS OUT
Our Opinions About Politicians

According to a bipartisan survey commission by the Project on Campaign Conduct:

- Fifty-nine percent believe that all or most candidates deliberately twist the truth.
- Thirty-nine percent believe that all or most candidates deliberately lie to voters.
- Forty-three percent believe that most or all candidates deliberately make unfair attacks on their opponents.
- Sixty-seven percent say they can trust the government in Washington only some of the time or never.
- Eighty-seven percent are concerned about the level of personal attacks in today's political campaigns.

The message we get and the interpretation we make from watching the way many of our political leaders operate is that you can't really tell people what you honestly think; you have to tell people both what they want to hear and what is in the best interests of the people who have the power to get you elected—certain voters, corporate lobbyists, political party insiders, media pundits, and more. I assume that most politicians get into public service to make a difference and to help their city, county, state, or nation. However, in most cases, it seems that the system is set up to force them to sell out on what's most important to them in service of grabbing more power, getting elected, or having "real" influence.

Another great political movie, which came out in 1998, is called Bulworth. Warren Beatty, who wrote, directed, and starred in this movie, plays depressed Senator Bulworth from California, who decides to hire a hit man to kill him so that his family will get a huge life insurance payout. Knowing he will die within a few days, he goes out on the road and starts speaking his truth—from his heart, honestly, and in a very funny and entertaining way. His realness is so refreshing, people actually love it, and what ensues in the movie is both hilarious and at the same time sad, as it underscores the lack of authenticity in politics and the deep yearning that we all have for honest communication from our politicians, which we rarely get.

Media

Given the enormous nature of the media today, this may be the biggest culprit in the lack of authenticity we face in our culture. Even with the rise of "reality" TV in the past ten years (which as we all know rarely seems to depict actual reality), it seems that most of what we get fed to us through the many different forms of media these days is filled with superficial news, gossip, endless bickering, political opinions based on agenda and fear, and lots of negative messages about what's wrong with the world, other people, and us.

The advertising industry alone makes billions and billions of dollars telling us we're not good enough the way we are—we need to buy their products in order to look, feel, and be better. The entertainment news shows, gossip magazines, and celebrity blogs on the Internet—as well as the "mainstream" news's obsession with sensationalized stories about conflicts, addictions, and scandals—cause many people to pay more attention to what's happening with Britney Spears and her children, which politician or media personality made a politically incorrect statement, or whether Brad Pitt and Angelina Jolie are staying together or not, than to what's going on in their own lives, in their relationships, and within themselves.

The media as a whole don't seem to be all that interested in real truth, complexity, ambiguity or paradox—it's all about sound bites, hype, right versus left, drama, and simplicity at all costs. Our attention spans are shorter; there are many more channels, including popular online sites. All of this has caused more competition for ratings and consequent ad revenues.

According to the A. C. Nielsen Co., the average American watches more than four hours of television each day (or twenty-eight hours per week, or two months of nonstop TV watching per year). In a sixty-five-year life, that person will have spent nine years glued to the tube. Because the majority of what's on television these days lacks depth, truth, or authenticity, this has a *major* impact on us.

While I don't believe that most of the people involved in the media are motivated by bad intentions, we are each affected significantly by what we see, hear, and learn from them. As it relates to our ability (or in most cases inability) to be authentic, the overriding message we get from the media is that perception is reality, we should believe what we're told, and that to be happy and successful we need to fall into line with what's popular.

Unhealthy Messages

Through our institutions, the people in our lives, and our own interpretations, we grow up with and live in a culture that constantly reinforces many unhealthy messages that keep us trapped in our own inauthentic ways of thinking, speaking, and acting. Some of these messages are obvious and overt, while others are more subtle. Either way, they're insidious and can do real damage to us, our relationships, and our ability to be genuine. Let's take a look at what some of these messages are and how they have an impact on us.

Be a Good Boy or Girl
Whether we heard it from our parents, our teachers, or other adults, all of us were taught both directly and

indirectly while growing up to be a "good boy" or a "good girl." This usually meant for us to do the things that the adults around us wanted us to do—go to bed, sit up straight, clean up after ourselves, play nice and share with the other kids, put smiles on our faces, and much more. However, many of us continue throughout our lives, long after we've left school and moved out of our parent's homes, to hear and respond to this message. We have the "disease to please"—always trying to do or say things that we think will make others like us and think we're "good."

While it was important and essential that the people raising us gave us certain rules and boundaries—to keep us safe and so that we had some important structure in life, this good boy or girl message taught us at an early age that who we are is based on how we behave. Underneath that was a message that we weren't good enough just as we were, we had to keep earning our love, approval, and appreciation from others, and in order to do so we had to live up to specific, subjective expectations of what it meant to be "good."

Any of us who have or still suffer from the disease to please (as I sometimes do) know how stressful, painful, and ultimately unfulfilling it can be. Constantly trying to do or say the "right" thing so that others will approve of us, like us, and keep us in good favor does not empower us to be ourselves, speak our truth, or live our deepest passions.

Anita, a former coaching client of mine, was constantly on the go, struggled to keep her life in balance, and was always dealing with lots of "family drama," as she would put it. As a single, young professional in her late twenties, she was doing pretty well in the first few years in her career in sales. She said she liked her work, but seemed bored, anxious, and discontented when she talked about her life, career, and relationships in our coaching sessions. A lot of her stress and suffering centered around her relationship with her father. He had always pushed her to succeed, and as a very successful businessman himself, he had high expectations for Anita.

In one of our sessions, when Anita was expressing some specific frustrations with her job and life, I challenged her to think about some other options for what she could do. The mere suggestion of her doing something else made her stop in her tracks. She said, "Are you kidding, I can't quit my job, my dad would kill me."

Anita, like so many of us, was attached to the opinions, expectations, and ideas of her father and other important people in her life. The options she saw for herself fit only into the category of what would have her be a "good girl" in his eyes. Although she did make some great progress in our time working together, her ability to create the kind of success and fulfillment in her career, relationships, and life that she truly wanted was significantly diminished by her attachment to pleasing her father.

Shut Up

Many of us were and still are told to "shut up." Sadly, this message was often communicated directly and with anger, shame, and resentment when we were young—particularly if we grew up in a dysfunctional or overtly negative home. Even for those of us who didn't hear these specific words or didn't grow up in a hostile environment, this message was and is all over the place in our lives and in our culture.

We all have learned that there are certain times and places when and where it is "appropriate" for us to speak up, but in most cases and when it comes to us truly speaking our minds, we learn to keep quiet and mind our own business. Think of the various phrases we've heard many times:

- "Children should be seen and not heard."
- "You can't say that."
- "Speak only when spoken to."
- "No side conversations."
- "Wait your turn."
- "Don't talk back."
- "Who do you think you are?"
- "Don't interrupt."
- "Be quiet."

These and so many other things were said to us as children, and variations of them continue to be said to us in our relationships, at work, and throughout our lives. Some of these things were said with good intentions, and our parents, teachers, and family members were telling this stuff to us as a way to set us up for success in life. However, the way that most of us interpreted these messages as children and then throughout life was and is that we're supposed to keep our mouths shut so as to not get in trouble.

I was recently delivering a seminar on conflict resolution skills to a group of leaders within one of my corporate clients, and as we were discussing the importance of honesty and straightforwardness as it related to being able to resolve issues, most everyone in the room was nodding their heads in agreement.

Charlie, one of the senior people in the room, raised his hand and said, "This all makes sense and is essential when dealing with my team, but it doesn't work with my own boss. You can't really be honest and speak your mind with upper management." As I looked around the room, I saw most of the heads nodding in agreement.

This was not so much a reflection of the dysfunction of this particular company, it was more a statement of how we continue to perpetuate the notion of "shutting up" throughout our lives, regardless of our level of experience, success, or responsibility.

Why Can't You Be More Like . . .

Another damaging message we get when we're young is that we should be more like someone else—our sibling, cousin, friend, classmate, famous kid on TV, or others. In moments of frustration our parents or teachers would see us doing something we weren't "supposed" to be doing, and in their infinite wisdom they thought that by pointing out how good someone else was at something, it would motivate us to be more how they wanted us to be. They would say things like,

"Why can't you be more like your sister? She sits at the table, eats her vegetables, and doesn't throw her food on the floor."

Questions like this may have seemed benign to our parents or teachers, and in fact what they said had some merit and truth to it at the time, but most of us heard these messages and interpreted them to mean we were not okay as we were, we should be like other kids, and there must be something wrong with us. In other words, we began to feel ashamed and guilty for being who we were.

Even for the kids who were often used as the "models," these messages were and still are damaging. If you were or are someone about whom other people say, "Why can't you be more like him or her?" it puts an enormous amount of pressure on you to continue to be the "ideal" person and someone that people hold in high esteem in this regard. No one wins this comparison game, and it sets us all up to act in ways that aren't genuine.

Susie and Jim, some friends of our friends whom we've spent time with on a couple of occasions, have three boys: Tyler, who is seven; Ryan, who is five; and Zackary, who is two and a half. The boys are full of passion and vigor, as many little boys their age are. They like to play, wrestle, and run around together. Susie and Jim, however, have the most trouble with Ryan. He constantly fights with his brothers and is very defiant, which causes a great deal of stress and frustration for everyone in the house.

As self-proclaimed "old school" parents, Susie and Jim are quite strict with their boys—they spank them occasionally, have very clearly defined rules, and run a "tight ship" in their house. So they reprimand Ryan, spank him often, and take him away from his brothers regularly for "time outs." In addition, they say to him many times a day, "Can't you just follow the rules and do what you're supposed to do like your brothers?"

While Jim and Susie clearly love Ryan and are doing what they think is best for him, it's obvious that these messages and their treatment are perpetuating much of the behavior they want to see change and keeping this challenging dynamic in place.

Calm Down

This is one that has always triggered me a great deal. Being told to "calm down" is something that we hear not only as children but throughout our lives—especially if we happen to be emotional, passionate, outspoken, opinionated, or all of the above, like me. If you want to really push my buttons, all you have to do is say to me "calm down" or make some reference to me overreacting, getting too emotional, or being too intense. As you can probably tell, this has happened to me many times throughout my life, and I am still a little sensitive about it. Ah, to be human!

We all get messages from the time we come into this world about when, how, and what is appropriate for us to express in terms of our emotions. Watch how people react to babies crying, which is something I've had quite a bit of personal experience with in the past three years. Parents, friends, grandparents, and even strangers passing by usually see a crying baby as a "bad" thing. Everyone has to do whatever they can to get the baby to stop crying as soon as possible. My feeling about a baby crying is different. Sure there are times when a baby is upset and needs help, food, changing, and so on. I'm not a huge fan of the sound of either of my girls crying, and I don't want them to suffer needlessly. However, I think oftentimes babies are just expressing themselves, and because they don't have much of a vocabulary at first, crying is one of the most passionate and appropriate ways for them to do that.

Our obsession with making sure a baby stops crying is usually more about us being uncomfortable with intense emotion, not liking the actual sound of the crying, not wanting other people to judge us for having an upset baby, and mostly some unconscious beliefs about which emotions are acceptable and appropriate and which ones are not, than it really is about taking care of the baby.

This same phenomenon goes on throughout our lives, long after we're babies. In our culture, most of the people around us do not encourage the passionate expression of many of our emotions, especially the ones that are considered "bad," such as anger, fear, sadness, hurt, shame, guilt, grief, sorrow, and others. Excitement, joy, love, happiness, and gratitude are okay, but they're often met with cynicism, and even these "good" ones are only encouraged to be expressed in "appropriate" ways and for "appropriate" reasons. In other words, whether we're upset or excited, we've been trained to "calm down" and not get too worked up one way or another.

Not being aware of, being comfortable with, or feeling as though we have "permission" to feel and express our true emotions can create debilitating suppression within us. Not knowing how to honor or express our emotions in an effective and productive way is even worse. This dynamic creates a great deal of stress and pressure, and it causes us to live our lives in an inauthentic way.

A lot of the negative behavior, unhealthy habits, and ultimate pain in our lives stems from our inability to acknowledge and express our intense emotions. While there are many factors that lead to things such as alcoholism, overeating, infidelity, eating disorders, workaholism, depression, and even suicide or violent crimes, one of the main underlying reasons is that we don't feel as though we're allowed or able to express the real feelings we have, and therefore do damage to ourselves and others.

Most recovering addicts will tell you that the reason they started and continued to abuse drugs or alcohol was self-medication, due to some specific emotion or emotions that they were unable to tolerate or deal with effectively. They'll also tell you that letting go of the actual substance of their addiction was the first step in their healing and growth process, but not in any way the last or most important one. Until they deal with the underlying issues and emotions that led them to the addiction, the real problems remain.

It's Better to Look Good Than to Feel Good

The message that appearance is more important than substance is all over the place in our culture. From our obsession with physical beauty and youth to the preoccupation we have with material possessions and outward success, many of us are striving to "make it" and to look good to others.

I've often found it interesting and somewhat annoying that at gatherings or when we run into people, the first question we often ask or are asked is, "What are you up to?" Not that I'm not interested in what other people are up to, I actually am. I just find it fascinating that we immediately talk about our careers, activities, vacations, families, plans, events, and so on, and often don't ask or talk about stuff that is more real—our feelings, our dreams, our struggles, our passions, and more. We focus on what we are doing instead of how we are truly feeling.

The messages from the media and elsewhere telling us that happiness is about losing weight and having a nice body, driving a fancy car, taking a nice vacation, having an attractive spouse, retiring early, owning a big home, doing the things that famous people do all reinforce that looking good on the outside is more important than feeling good on the inside. Even many people who are aware of this, like me, still struggle with it all the time.

I catch myself more often than I'd like to admit obsessing about my physical appearance, focusing on my external success, worrying how other people perceive me and how I'm doing, and trying to portray a sense of confidence and fulfillment, instead of paying attention to actually feeling that way inside. As my work has expanded and I've become more public, this has actually become even more challenging for me. As I often say and will probably reiterate a few times throughout this book, we teach best what we most need to learn.

Questions to Ponder

As we move to Chapter Two, and then ultimately into the five principles of authenticity, pay attention to all of the institutions, programming, and messages from the past still having an impact on you today that make it challenging for you to be yourself, speak your truth, and live in an authentic way. Ask yourself how all of this continues to affect you on a personal level.

The following questions are for you to think about or write answers to, as a way of making this more real and specific for you and your life:

1. What have you learned from family, school, religion, politics, media, or others about being yourself?
2. What specific messages did you receive growing up that made it difficult for you to be authentic?
3. What specific institutions, influences, or messages in your life today get in the way of your fully being yourself and living an authentic life?

As you consider your answers to these questions, you should be able to see clearly how much impact these institutions, influences, and messages have on you and your ability (or inability) to be authentic.

We are not victims of our culture, family, or any of the things we have been taught in the past or are currently reminded of in the present. It is, however, essential that you acknowledge these influences, so that you can admit them, own them, and ultimately take responsibility for how you have internalized these messages and why it can be difficult for you to be authentic.

Now that we've looked at some of the most pervasive external factors that make authenticity challenging for us, we're ready to take a look at the more insidious and damaging aspects of all of this—our own false personas, self-criticism, and fear.

2

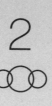

i can't say or
do that

"God has given you one face, and you make
yourself another."

—William Shakespeare

N ow that we've taken a look at some of the family influences, cultural institutions, and societal
messages that can make it challenging for us to be
authentic, let's turn inward and look at the more personal
reasons why we often struggle to be ourselves.

The intensity of our life circumstances does play a
role in this process. However, the way we personally inter-
pret these circumstances and how we internalize what we

see, hear, and experience has everything to do with how we show up in life and engage with others and ourselves. In other words, it's not so much what happens to us, but how we react and the decisions we make about ourselves and life that cause us to be inauthentic.

For us to be true to ourselves, to live with authenticity, and to go for what we really want in life, we have to first acknowledge, own, and take responsibility for our own self-imposed limitations, our phony ways of being and acting, and the specific things that make it hard for us to be ourselves. To survive in life, each of us has created a "persona"—invented so as to hide the "unacceptable," flawed, and scared aspects of whom we think we are that we don't want others to see.

In this chapter we'll look at why we created our personas and what impact they have, how we criticize and compare ourselves to others in a debilitating way, and what specifically we're afraid of as it relates to being ourselves and living an authentic life. Our ability to address these things directly with honesty and compassion is what allows us to move beyond our limits and to experience the freedom that authenticity provides. We have to first tell the truth about why we don't tell and live our truth in order to live in a way that is real.

The Creation of Our Personas

The concept of the "persona" was introduced and popularized by psychologist Carl Jung in the early twentieth century. According to Jung, a persona is an individual's social facade or front—the role that an individual plays in life or in particular situations. We each have a certain persona that we've created to "make it" in life. In some cases we've done this in a very conscious way and are aware of it. And in other cases, this process is more unconscious—both its creation and perpetuation. In either case, our personas help us cope with childhood pain and drama, as well as our own personal fears and insecurities as we move through life. However, the more developed our personas are and the more attached we are to the roles we play in life, the more difficult it is for us to be authentic. It's important that we identify and confront our personas and see them for what they really are, inauthentic social masks we wear.

At its best, a persona can be the good impression we wish to present to others. But it can also be the false impression we use to manipulate people. At its worst, it can be mistaken, even by ourselves, for our true nature. Sometimes even we believe we are what we pretend to be, which makes it difficult if not impossible for us to be real.

Learning to Survive

As we discussed in Chapter One, there are many external influences that teach us directly and indirectly about how to be and act in life—family, school, organized religion, politics, the media, and more all send us messages (be good, shut up, be more like others, calm down, look good, and so on) that we internalize and have to make sense of as we grow and evolve in our lives. Because so much of what we learn and how we learn it is based on inauthentic notions and shallow ideas, and is taught to us by others who struggle to be themselves as well, we each have to figure out how best to survive in the given situations and with the specific circumstances of our lives. Many of us who end up creating "success" as kids, in school, and as we move through life into adulthood are simply better at faking it than others.

A persona, which is initially created when we're young, is one of the most important survival techniques we use. It's what we want to be known as, not what or who we really are. We develop this persona in order to get love or attention, and to have people like us—our parents, siblings, teachers, friends, and others. As we grow and develop, our personas may change and evolve (although they often stay fairly consistent), but the key elements and ultimate goals are the same—hide who I really am and help me get what I want. This is all an appropriate and important part of our development as human beings. There is nothing "wrong" with us for having a persona. However, as we evolve and want to step into new realms of success and fulfillment in life, we usually have to confront our personas in a more authentic way, so that we can move beyond their limits and become more of who we really are.

Joe, one of my clients, is a really funny guy. He makes everyone laugh and has a wonderful sense of humor. However, he acknowledges that oftentimes when he gets scared, doesn't want to deal with something, or is in a new or uncomfortable situation, he cracks lots of jokes as an automatic reaction. He said he began to do this as a kid because with so many siblings and lots of chaos in his house, this was how he was able to stand out and also how he could survive when things got hard, scary, and even painful growing up. Joe's sense of humor, which can be real and authentic at times, is often part of his persona—always having to be "the funny guy" in situations, especially as a way to hide his fear, insecurity, and other real feelings which might make him feel vulnerable. Through our work together, Joe was able to identify more aspects of his persona, like his humor, and with this deeper understanding he can choose to be funny in a more real and authentic way, and not *have* to be as a way to cover up his anxiety and awkwardness.

Dealing with Pain

My parents split up when I was three. My dad's bipolar disorder and some deep-seated issues and conflicts between my mom and him forced the end of their ten-year marriage. It was 1977; my mom had been raised in the 1940s and 1950s as a Catholic schoolgirl in a small town in Rhode Island. I assume one of the last things she wanted to be was a single mom of two young children—but that's what happened. She also had not worked in eight years when she and my dad split up, which had been one of the main points of contention in their marriage—my mom wanted to go back to work but my dad wanted her to stay home. Ultimately, it was my mom's decision to end their relationship—even though things weren't good between them, my dad didn't want to leave. My mom stood up for herself, and although

I'm sure she was scared, she did what she thought was best for her and us by asking my dad to go.

Over the next few years, things were challenging and scary for me and in our house. I didn't understand why my parents weren't together anymore. My dad moved into an apartment a few miles away from our house in Oakland. It was fun to visit him, but confusing. I knew my mom and my older sister Lori were both upset, and so was my dad, but I didn't fully get what was going on.

By 1979, after a few unsuccessful attempts at recon-ciliation by my dad, it was obvious to him and to us that my parents weren't getting back together. My dad had moved across the bay to be even closer to San Francisco, where he worked as a radio announcer. Although we went to see him every other weekend, things began to change for the worse, and he became more angry and despondent. By 1981 he'd fallen into a deep depression, by 1982 he'd lost his job and his apartment, and over the next five years he was in and out of halfway houses, hospitals, hotels, and other strange places—often we didn't know for months at a time where he was or if he was okay.

Needless to say, this was quite painful for me and my sister, and for my mom as well—who was struggling to make ends meet, and take care of us, without any support, financial or otherwise, from my father.

As all of this played out, it had a significant impact on my development as young boy. Much of my persona, as is true for many of us, was created in those first few years of my life. While I was not fully aware of it at the time, when my dad left and with all of the ensuing pain and uncertainty that followed for me and my family, I made some decisions and started to act and be certain ways to try to make up for this—both at home and at school. I took on the role of making others happy—my family and friends. In addition, I decided that in order to make things better I would succeed, achieve, and perform. Much of my focus in school and later in sports became about being the "best" and always achieving at the highest possible level. I figured that if I could do well enough, maybe it would make things okay for me and my family, and maybe it would help take away some of the pain and embarrassment that we felt based on the situation with my parent's divorce, our home and financial circumstances, and my dad's mental illness.

People who come from more traditional families (that is, no divorce, outward "dysfunction," and so on), or ones that on the surface seem to be "healthy" or "normal," often have to deal with a lot of unspoken pain—abuse that is hidden, infidelity that is never addressed or dealt with, unexpressed emotions, lack of communication, and much more.

In some of the most extreme cases, people go even further than the creation of a persona, as we've been discussing it here, and actually invent what is known in psychology as a "false self." This concept, popularized in the mid-twentieth century by psychologist Donald Winnicott, is often associated with people who have dealt with major childhood trauma that resulted in abuse or abandonment. The creation of the false self is understood to be a defense mechanism established to protect one from the trauma and abuse of his or her life. Those with extreme versions of this false self can literally be pathological or completely out of touch with reality.

While all of this exists on a continuum from a somewhat benign persona to a demented and debilitating false self, we all have invented phony ways of being and acting in life to survive, deal with our pain, and get by. These false ways of being and acting have an enormous impact on our lives, our relationships, and our ability (or in most cases inability) to be authentic.

Compensating for Something We Think We Lack

We create a public mask or identity to cover up what we don't want people to see about us. Like putting makeup on our faces, we hope that our personas will hide the "blemishes" we think we have as human beings. The problem is, however, this never works. When we live and act exclusively in our personas, even if we're able to achieve what we think are positive outcomes, relationships, and situations in our lives, it only reinforces our insecurity. The more we operate as our personas, the more we train ourselves to believe that who we are naturally is not good enough.

Some of the aspects of our personas, in and of themselves and when exhibited in an authentic way, can be positive. Being funny, likeable, outgoing, smart, charismatic, polite, kind, independent, resourceful, helpful, creative, action-oriented, caring, giving, passionate, and more can be wonderful. However, in order for us to have the freedom, power, and fulfillment that come with any of these (and other) positive qualities, we have to own them and express them authentically, not use them to compensate for something we think is wrong with us.

EXERCISE
Understanding and Owning Your Persona

Part 1

Take out a piece of paper or your journal. At the top of the paper write, "My Persona." Take some time to think about and write about your own persona. What "mask" do you wear in public? What things do you feel you have to do or say at work, in social settings, and in general so that people will think of you in a positive way or so they won't find out some of the "bad" things about you that you don't want them to know?

Part 2

List some of the key elements or specific traits of your persona that you've identified and see if you can acknowledge, without judging yourself, what each of these characteristics are hiding. For example, you may be someone who is allegedly "happy" and "positive," but as you look at that from this perspective you realize that this actually covers up some of your deep-seated anger, fear, or negativity. Or you may be "independent," which is hiding your fear of being alone or your inability to trust others.

Part 3: *Assessment*

What did you uncover about yourself doing this exercise? How honest were you with yourself and about your persona? How can you use this to become more of who you really are? Acknowledging the specific aspects of your persona and then telling the truth about what they're specifically hiding can be liberating and can give you access to being more real.

As we become more aware of our own personas and are able to recognize them, without judgment, we can have compassion for ourselves and at the same time begin to live, speak, act, and be more authentic. Our ability to be ourselves and live authentic lives is directly related to our own awareness of when and how we're being inauthentic. Once we notice and take responsibility for being phony, we can then choose to be more real or not. It's up to us, always—as long as we're aware and honest.

Self-Criticism

Many of us are our own worst enemies. We spend a great deal of time and energy criticizing ourselves. Another main reason we have a hard time being who we are and being authentic in life is that we think who we are is flawed or at least needs a great deal of improvement. Self-criticism is one of the most pervasive and insidious ways we sell out and sabotage ourselves.

The "Gremlin"

We each have our own personal Gremlin. You may have heard it called by other names: inner critic, negative ego, inner voice, or something else. The Gremlin is the voice in our heads made up of all the negative and critical thoughts we have about ourselves on a regular basis.

Many of us are very familiar with our own Gremlin— he or she is a constant companion, and we know that "voice" whenever we hear it. Some of us are not as familiar with our own Gremlin; we actually think that the negative thoughts and ideas coming from our Gremlins are actually true. First, it's important for us to acknowledge, once again with compassion, that we each have a Gremlin, and second it's important for each of us to create a relationship with our Gremlin so that it no longer runs our life.

If you want to come face to face with your Gremlin and hear what it sounds like, just pay attention to the voice in your head when you're thinking about doing something new or different, when you're in an unfamiliar situation, when you're going for something that really matters to you, or when you're taking a risk of any kind—big or small. In many cases, your Gremlin is right there to criticize you, point out your weaknesses, remind you that you could fail and embarrass yourself, and in general sabotage your ability to take action with confidence.

Sadly, most of us give away our power and ultimately our lives to our Gremlins. Our Gremlins aren't interested in our success or happiness, all they're interested in is our survival in the moment. Our Gremlins often say or ask things like

- "You can't do that."
- "Who do you think you are?"
- "Everyone will laugh at you."
- "Remember the last time you tried something like this and what a mess you made of that?"
- "Why do you always say and do such stupid stuff?"
- "You don't have what it takes."

These accusatory statements and questions, and many others like them, come from our Gremlins all the time. As you read this, I'm sure you can recognize the negative impact your Gremlin has on your life, your self-esteem, your goals, your success, and, most specifically, your ability to be yourself. Your Gremlin doesn't want you to live an authentic life, speak your truth, express your real emotions, go for what you want, or celebrate who you are. It relishes in your self-criticism, doubt, and limitation.

Not Good Enough

The bottom-line message we get from our Gremlins and that many of us experience throughout our lives, is that we are *not good enough*. This idea that we are not good enough, which for many of us has become a core belief we have about ourselves and also the source of motivation for many aspects of our lives (even our own desire to learn, grow, pick up a book like this, and more), is incredibly damaging and painful. As difficult as this can be, it's also one of the most universal experiences for us as humans. While some of us may think and feel as though we aren't good enough more intensely than others, very few people have completely transcended this type of thinking and feeling altogether. Even though we don't usually go around openly admitting that we don't feel good enough in various areas of our lives, it shows up in many of the things we say and do, or in the things we choose not to say and do.

For example, Rich hired me to coach him specifically to be a more effective leader. He'd spent many years as a successful insurance agent and was quite an accomplished professional. The company he worked for acknowledged his success by giving him his first leadership role. Within a short time he had a direct report team of about ten people and an office of almost forty that he oversaw. He was excited by the challenge of this new job, but overwhelmed by the responsibility he now had at work, in addition to his responsibility at home with his wife and two kids. As we worked together for a few months, it became clear that Rich's main issue was not about leadership, time management, or even stress management—all things he constantly asked me about and read about in the popular business magazines he regularly devoured. His main challenge was that he was convinced he was not good enough. No matter what happened, he was never satisfied.

When I challenged him on this, and suggested that he take some time to appreciate what was going well, or even just asked him to tell me some things he thought he was good at, Rich had very little to say. Whenever we talked about his issues, challenges, and areas in which he thought he could improve, he couldn't stop talking. Rich said to me one day, "What has made me successful in life is always improving on my weak points—that's what got me here and what I need to do to stay at the top of my game."

I agreed with Rich that improving on certain areas in which he was not as strong as he could be was a good idea for him, as can be for all of us as we grow and evolve in life. However, if our core belief is that we're not good enough and that there's something inherently wrong with us, as it was for Rich and also is for many others as well, no matter how much we "improve" or achieve in life, it'll never be enough and will always reinforce our feelings of inadequacy.

The progress and success Rich ultimately made in our coaching sessions, and in his life and career in general, had a lot less to do with him "improving" on his areas of weakness and more about him noticing his tendency to think and feel he was "not good enough" and then to slowly but surely pay more attention to what he was doing well, his skills and talents, and the things he appreciated about himself. He became more honest and real about his true strengths and weaknesses, and stopped using his fear of inadequacy as a source of motivation—something which many of us do in an unconscious way.

One simple way this shows up in our lives on a regular basis is in all of the expectations and demands we place on ourselves for how we "should" be. Some people like to call this "should-ing" on yourself. What usually lies underneath these "shoulds," for me and almost everyone I know or work with, is a feeling that we aren't good enough just as we are and that until we do all of the things or be all of the ways we think we *should* be, we aren't okay.

EXERCISE
I Should . . .

Part 1
Take out a piece of paper or your journal. On the top of the paper write, "I Should . . ." Then take some time to make a list of all of the things you think you should do or say, or ways you should be in your life right now that you think you aren't. For example, "I should be more patient," "I should get more sleep," "I should be more organized," "I should eat more healthy food and exercise more regularly," "I should spend more quality time with the people I love," and so on.

Part 2
Read back over your list and circle the BIG ONES, the top five or so "shoulds" that you give the most attention to.

Part 3: *Assessment*
How much time and energy do you spend thinking about what you "should" do and ultimately feeling like you aren't

good enough? However much or little it is, it's important to acknowledge and own this, as it's one of the most insidious ways we stop ourselves from being who we really are. Although some of the items on our list of "shoulds" may truly be things that are important for us to do or ways to be, when we relate to them only from this perspective, we shame ourselves and reinforce our feelings of inadequacy, which, while understandable and encouraged by many people and influences around us, is not ultimately a healthy or productive way to motivate ourselves.

Comparing Ourselves to Others

Another big thing we do that stops us from being who we are and living with authenticity is comparing ourselves to others—the people around us, the people on TV and in the magazines, and even ourselves from the past (that is, feeling as though we're not as good as we used to be—one I often struggle with big time myself).

We live in a competitive society, and from a very early age we learn to compete with our siblings, classmates, friends, and others. Most of us also learn when we're young—and as we get older as well—that being better than those around us is an important way to succeed and feel good about ourselves. So often we define our success or failure on the basis of the relative success or failure of those around us (in other words, how we measure up).

In September of 1995 I was home after my first summer of playing minor league baseball. I'd gotten drafted that

June and played my first three months of pro baseball for two minor league affiliates in the Kansas City Royals organization. One of my friends, Jeremy, who was two years ahead of me in school and had been a teammate of mine at Stanford, got called up to the Major Leagues that September to pitch for the Chicago White Sox. I was fired up when I saw they were coming to town to play the Oakland A's and that Jeremy was scheduled to pitch. He got me tickets and I went to the game. Although Jeremy didn't have a very good game and the Sox lost, it was so exciting to see him, my former teammate and friend, pitching live in a Major League game—especially at the Oakland Coliseum where I'd watched hundreds of games growing up as a kid.

After the game I went back to the team hotel to meet up with Jeremy and his fiancée in the bar for a drink and a bite. When I got there, the two of them looked pretty down. As we started talking, I could tell that Jeremy's performance and the outcome of the game had upset them both quite a bit. As a competitive baseball player myself, and fellow pitcher, I could relate to being disappointed and frustrated after a bad outing. But to me it was so incredibly exciting that Jeremy was up in the Big Leagues and that he'd been given a chance to start against the A's, I couldn't understand why he was so upset. As we talked further, I realized that it was all relative, and that just like me getting upset after a bad game—in high school, college, or the minor leagues—when we spend most of our time and place most of our attention on competition and comparison, which is what so much of sports and our culture are all about, our success and how we feel about ourselves are almost always contingent upon how well we perform and how we do in relation to others.

Ironically, as we continued to talk that night at the bar, I asked Jeremy what it was like to be making so much money. At the time the Major League minimum salary was $109,000, which, pro-rated over the course of the season, came out to a little more than $14,000 per month, or $7,000 each check (every two weeks). For a guy who was twenty-three years old at the time, just two years out of college baseball, and already pitching in the Major Leagues, this seemed like a lot of money, especially to me, who'd never had much money in my life and had just finished my first pro season in which I made the minor league minimum salary of $850 per month. Jeremy's response surprised me: he said, "It really isn't all that much money."

"Really?" I replied.

"When you're around guys who are making four or five million dollars a year and living the million-dollar lifestyle, it kind of puts it all in perspective," he said.

Once again I saw that it's all relative. While I was sitting there jealous of Jeremy, who as a fellow left-handed pitcher was doing exactly what I wanted to be doing—pitching in the Major Leagues—he was probably looking at or thinking about someone else on his team who was making lots more money, who had already established himself as a successful big leaguer, and whom he wanted to be like. I just as easily could've been talking to a high school kid who would have been jealous of me for getting a scholarship to Stanford and for playing in the minor leagues with the Kansas City Royals organization. When we compare ourselves to others and define who we are on the basis of how we think we measure up to those around us, not only does everyone ultimately lose, we aren't able to have any real sense of who we are; what's important; or what the value of our own talent, success, and uniqueness is.

Another interesting example of this in our culture today is the obsession with celebrity and fortune. As we discussed in Chapter One when we talked about the influence of the media and our fascination with celebrity gossip and sensationalized stories about famous people, the rise of the information age and all of the ways in which younger people have been able to gain fame and fortune have been intensified in recent years. Eighty-one percent of eighteen-to twenty-five-year-olds surveyed in a 2007 Pew Research Center poll said getting rich is their most important or second most important life goal; fifty-one percent said the same about being famous. Sadly, many of us in our culture, regardless of our age, think that if we're able to get famous or at least create financial wealth, we'll be happy and fulfilled. Even with literally thousands of examples to the contrary, many of us are holding our breath, hoping that one day we'll "make it" and then things will work out for us. As we do this, we just continue to reinforce that who we are is not as good as others, and this becomes yet another thing that gets in the way of being ourselves.

Criticizing Our Bodies and Appearance

One specific area in which many of us struggle to accept and appreciate who and how we are is our bodies. Many people, myself included, are super critical of how they look and of the size, shape, and appearance of their bodies. Over the course of my life, some of my deepest pain and self-loathing has had to do with me feeling ugly, flawed, or simply not good enough physically. We live in a culture that has an obsession with appearance and with "body beautiful." And while there's nothing wrong with us wanting take care of ourselves and wanting to look good physically, I think that many of us go way overboard with this. We forget that our ability to appreciate our bodies and feel good about our appearance isn't based on how much we weigh, how tall we are, the size of certain body parts, how our skin looks, how much hair we have (a big one for me these days), or anything else. It all has to do with how we *feel* about our bodies and how we look.

No body is perfect. All bodies change with time. We shouldn't expect to look the same at forty as we did at twenty, or at sixty-five as we did when we were forty-five. A sad but true example of this is eating disorders. Eating disorders, such as anorexia nervosa, bulimia nervosa, and binge eating, are becoming increasingly prevalent throughout Western countries. According to U.S. estimates from The National Institute of Mental Health, between 5 and 10 percent of girls and women (five to ten million people) and one million boys and men suffer from eating disorders.

Estimates suggest that as many as 15 percent of young women adopt unhealthy attitudes and behaviors about food. In addition,

- An estimated ten percent of female college students suffer from a clinical or subclinical (borderline) eating disorder.
- An estimated one in one hundred American women binges and purges to lose weight.
- Fifteen percent of young women have significantly disordered eating attitudes and behavior.
- Studies suggest that five to ten percent of people with anorexia or bulimia are males.
- An estimated one in three of all dieters develops compulsive dieting attitudes and behaviors.
- Each day Americans spend an average of $109 million on dieting and diet-related products.

These sobering statistics show us the pervasive and damaging nature of this specific type of self-criticism. These numbers address those who have gone to the extreme and actually developed an eating disorder, but they don't address the less significant issues that many of us have about our bodies, appearance, and overall sense of ourselves. Being critical of our bodies and of our appearance is yet another way we diminish ourselves, think we aren't good enough, and hold ourselves back from being who we really are.

CHECK THIS OUT
Statistics About Cosmetic Procedures

There were nearly 11.7 million surgical and nonsurgical cosmetic procedures performed in the United States in 2007, as reported by the American Society for Aesthetic Plastic Surgery (ASAPS). Since 1997, there has been a 457 percent increase in the total number of cosmetic procedures (up from 2.1 million in 1997).

- Fifty-six percent of women say they approve of cosmetic surgery.
- Fifty-seven percent of men say they approve of cosmetic surgery.

Fear

The third and probably most significant personal reason that being authentic is hard for us—in addition to our personas and our self-criticism—is fear.

When it comes right down to it, the reason that many of us don't do or say what is true for us is that we're scared. We worry about failing, being rejected, disappointing others, being judged, and much more. We also worry, ironically, about succeeding.

Let's take a look at some of these specific fears and how they stop us from being ourselves. As we go through these, think about some of the real fears you have about being fully authentic. We all have fears, especially when it comes to being real. The more honest and aware we are about our own fears and blocks, the more easily we can move beyond them.

Failure

Just the word *failure* can send shivers down our spines. If you're like me, most of the people I know, and many of my clients, you're probably not a big fan of failing. Most of us have had some big failures in our lives, and many of these have been painful, disappointing, and hard to swallow. Sadly, as we move through life, we often give away our power, passion, and authenticity to failure or, more specifically, our fear of failure. Many of us are too scared to do or say the things that are most true and important to us because we aren't sure how they'll turn out ultimately.

Michael Jordan said, "I missed one hundred percent of the shots I did not take." While this great quote can be used to motivate and inspire us to take courageous action, many of us choose not to shoot, deciding that our fear of missing and the impact of that is more important than making it.

As I was preparing to write this book, I began to ask some specific questions of the people around me—friends, family members, clients, and others. One of the specific questions I asked was, "Think of a time in your life when you 'sold out' on your deepest truth and did not do or say something you really wanted to do. . . . What got in your way and what impact did this have on you and your life?"

The responses I got back from people to this particular question were fascinating, honest, and enlightening. A common theme I continued to hear from many people was fear. Here's one of those responses. Steve said,

> I had been accepted into a Ph.D. program. My friends gathered and gave me a going away party. The day that I was scheduled to leave, I didn't. I just didn't go. Fear entered me in a way that froze me and I made up some lies about why I couldn't leave my family, friends, etc. The truth was I collapsed into my fear about picking up my life to do next what I had always wanted to do. I just dropped the ball due to a fear of change and what that might bring.

Fear of failure can stop us in our tracks and render us frozen—unwilling to do or say what we know to be true in our hearts. How has your own fear of failure caused you to sell out on what's important to you in your life? How is your fear of failure affecting you and your ability to be authentic right now?

Success

As scared as we might be of failing, ironically, many of us are secretly even more afraid of succeeding. While fear of failure seems pretty straightforward, fear of success is a little more complex. Our reasons for being scared of success can vary from not enjoying the extra responsibility (for what it takes to create and maintain success and then what people will expect from us); not wanting to give up our struggle, stress, and negativity (even though we complain about these things, many of us secretly get off on the drama and self-pity at the same time); or worrying that people won't like us anymore (because we all love to make fun of and tear down people who succeed in our society).

Our fear of what might happen to us, what people might say about us, or how things would change in our lives and relationships if we did have real success, often keeps us not only from really going after the success itself but from doing and saying what we really want to. Think of the times in your life when you have consciously or unconsciously sabotaged your own success because you got scared or started to worry about the pressure and expectations that were beginning to build up. Also, think of times you have not shared something you were proud of or had accomplished, or didn't admit to having a specific goal or talent because you feared it would make others feel bad or then you'd be put on the spot and forced to "shine," which made you nervous. Our fear of success is sometimes harder to see than our fear of failure, but it's just as debilitating as it relates to our ability to be authentic and go for what we really want.

Rejection

I believe that the greatest fear we all have as human beings is the fear of being alone—no one to love us or care about us, or who is there for us. As a result of this fundamental fear of loneliness, we have many intense fears that we'll be rejected in relationships, business, and life. We often think about what we'll do, what we'll say, and specifically what requests we're willing to make of others based on our fear of what we expect the response to be. Because of this we often don't say what we really mean, don't ask for what we really want, or interact with others in an inauthentic way.

Our fear of rejection is so strong that we won't pick up the phone to call potential clients, won't ask people we're interested in out on a date, won't tell our spouse what we'd like as a gift or in the bedroom, and much more. We're even so sensitive and insecure about rejection that we worry about rejecting others and do and say odd things like, "It's me, not you," when ending a relationship. Another great response to my question about selling out came from Blake:

> One huge regret I have was how I handled the breakup with an ex-girlfriend of mine. We'd been dating for a little over a year, and I decided to break up with her over the phone. The idea was that it would be simpler and easier than flying to see her. I guess it was simpler—making a call—but it didn't feel right from the beginning, and I felt terrible about it afterwards. At a minimum, I owed it to her to see her face to face, but it was one of my biggest mistakes. While I still think that our relationship wasn't right long term, the way I handled our breakup was inauthentic and chicken. I still regret it to this day. (I actually think she still hates me—and I don't think she's in the wrong.)

Our fear of being rejected or feeling discomfort causes us to alter our words and actions, play safe, and try to manipulate people and situations so we get what we want without having to do, say, or ask for anything that might result in a rejection that'll hurt.

Disappointment

The flip side of our fear of rejection is often our fear of disappointing other people—letting them down. This one is also directly connected with our fear of failure and success. The bottom line is that we tend to worry a lot about disappointing the people in our lives, so much so that it can alter what we do and say and can contribute to our inauthentic ways of being.

Right before I met my wife Michelle, I dated a wonderful woman named Elizabeth. Although Elizabeth and I only dated for about six months, our relationship got very serious, very quickly. We met in April in San Francisco, where I was living. Elizabeth lived in Los Angeles. Within a month or two we were already talking about moving in together (in L.A.) and about our future—marriage, children, and so on. Even though it was all happening so fast and I was still pretty young, twenty six years old, it felt right and I was excited. As the next few months passed and I started to get more serious about making my plans to move to L.A. to be with Elizabeth, something started to change. I couldn't put my finger on it, but it was obvious to me and to her.

Elizabeth, who was a few years older than me and quite a wise and direct woman (which I really appreciated about her), kept saying, "Mike, if a relationship doesn't work out, it's because one or both people aren't telling the truth." She was right, and from what I could tell, she was being honest, open, and straightforward with me about her desires, concerns, and feelings. I thought I was as well. By the end of the summer, I had decided not to move to L.A., and Elizabeth and I ultimately decided, on good terms, to end our relationship.

In hindsight I could clearly see what had happened, although I wasn't fully aware of it at the time. I'd gotten so excited about being with Elizabeth, moving in with her, and planning a future with her, but when the "honeymoon" ended and reality set in, I realized that I wasn't ready and was totally scared about what was happening and how fast it had happened. I didn't know how at first to take responsibility for this, to deal with it directly, and to communicate it honestly to Elizabeth—especially since I'd already told her I was on board and excited about us moving forward with our relationship. As she so brilliantly understood, when things don't work out in relationships it's because one or both people don't understand the truth of what's happening or they aren't willing to be honest about it, for fear of disappointing the other person.

Judgments

The "granddaddy" of all of our fears—specifically as it relates to being authentic—is our fear of being judged. What will they think of me? What will they say? Will they still like me? Will I still fit in? Most of us secretly worry that if people really knew what we thought; our true beliefs; our deepest fears; our most important visions; and some of the weird, quirky, irrational things we thought or did—no one would like us or want to be around us anymore.

The irony, of course, is that this isn't true, and even though most of us know this, we still run scared and do lots of things to avoid being judged.

Here's a list of some of the things that our fear of being judged stops us from doing:

- Speaking our truth
- Disagreeing with someone "important"
- Standing up for what we believe in
- Admitting we don't know something, understand something, or like something we think we're "supposed" to
- Taking risks
- Changing our life circumstances—career, relationships, location, and so on
- Doing things differently than others around us—at work, at home, in our community, and so on
- Changing our minds
- Doing things we really want to do that we assume others won't like, understand, or approve of

These are just a few of the many examples of what we don't do or say because we fear other people's reactions or judgments. What is it that we're so afraid of? What do we worry that people will think, say, or do that is so scary to us? Most of the stuff that we worry others will judge us on is stuff we already judge so negatively about ourselves. Our Gremlins remind us all the time that we aren't good enough and point out all of the things we already think are flawed about us. Our fears of other people judging us are based on what we already see as our weaknesses and things we're already self-conscious about, for the most part. When we worry about being perceived as selfish, we usually already think that we are. When we worry that people will not like us, we're reacting to the place within us that already doesn't like ourselves.

A distorted view of our external world is always a reflection of our internal world. The main person we're scared to be judged by is ourselves. Ironically, we're constantly judging ourselves anyway; there's no need to be scared of it, since it happens all the time. Herein lies the paradox of the fear of judgment: we think we're worried about what others think about us, when we're really most vulnerable to damage from what we think about ourselves.

Questions to Ponder

As we move to Chapter Three and the five principles of authenticity, it's important for you to be aware of all of the things that get in your way of being yourself—that is, what makes being authentic hard for you personally. As you're able to acknowledge your own challenges with authenticity, with compassion, with honesty, and without judgment, you'll be able to access your own deeper truth more effectively and in so doing, be more of who you truly want to be in your life, your work, and your relationships.

As a way of wrapping up this important chapter and this first section of the book, here are a few questions for you to think about:

1. What are the biggest obstacles that get in your way of being real? (your persona, self-criticism, fear, and so on)
2. What are you most self critical about, and what impact does this have on your ability to be authentic? (competency, appearance, background, track record, education, status, and so on)
3. What are some of the biggest fears you have about the potential outcome of being fully yourself, speaking your truth, and going for what you truly want in life?

As you consider your answers to these questions, you should be able to see clearly how much your interpretation of the external forces and messages in your life, and your own personal belief system, affect you and your ability (or inability) to be authentic.

Noticing and owning our own inauthentic ways of being and acting is actually what gives us access to being more real in any given situation or relationship, and in the moment-by-moment experience of our lives. Be honest with yourself. Have compassion for yourself. This isn't easy, but it's important. And, know that the more willing and able you are to admit some of your own challenges and acknowledge places in your life where you're inauthentic, the more able you are in turn to be real. Now that we have looked honestly at some of the things that make it difficult for us to be ourselves, we're ready to move into the five principles of authenticity.

part two

☉

the five
principles of
authenticity

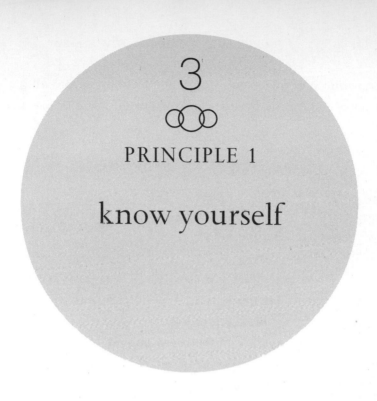

3

PRINCIPLE 1

know yourself

"Knowing others is wisdom, knowing yourself is enlightenment."

—Lao Tzu

The chapters in the next part of the book present the five principles of authenticity that I teach my clients, which are base on the personal growth work I've done with thousands of people and in my own life over the past fifteen years. These principles are designed to

provide specific insights, ideas, and techniques for living a
life of authenticity, freedom, and fulfillment. The principles are

1. Know Yourself
2. Transform Your Fear
3. Express Yourself
4. Be Bold
5. Celebrate Who You Are

These principles are specifically designed to show
you how to be more real in your relationships, your
work, and your life. Each one builds upon the one before
it, and together they create a new approach for how you
can tap into the true power of authenticity and transform
your life.

Knowing Who We Are

How well do you know yourself, I mean *really* know yourself? The first essential aspect of our journey to live a more
authentic life is to know who we truly are at the deepest
level. Some of us are more aware of ourselves than others.
Knowing ourselves, like being authentic itself, is a life-long
process. The more deliberate we are about this the more we
can grow and evolve.

The fact that you picked up this book and have read
it up to this point says something about who you are and
your willingness to know yourself. This is good news,

as willingness is one of the most important aspects of self-growth and discovery. However, given our depth, complexity, and constant evolution as human beings, it's not possible for us to get to a point in life at which we know *everything* about ourselves. In fact, the majority of us stay pretty unconscious and unaware of ourselves for much of our lives—which often causes a great deal of confusion and suffering for us and those around us. Our goal, therefore, is to continue to discover more and more about who we really are as we go through our journey. This first principle, Know Yourself, is a foundational piece of being who you truly are and having the courage to live, speak, and act in an authentic way.

Self-Awareness

Our journey toward deeper authenticity starts with our awareness of ourselves. There's a difference between knowing *about* yourself and actually being fully aware of yourself.

Knowing about yourself, while important, is much more about content and details and much less about real feelings and awareness. We know about ourselves by understanding facts and aspects of who we are, where we've been, what we've done, certain public qualities we have, and so on. Other ways we can describe knowing about ourselves are the "story" that we tell others about who we are, as well as the story that we tell ourselves—which, as we discussed in detail in the first part of the book, are often very different from one another. In either case, these "stories" aren't usually all that real and often are filled with lots of judgments, assessments, misrepresentations, and beliefs about who we think we are, who we want to be, or who we think we should be—not who we *really* are.

Being fully aware of ourselves is about looking more deeply within. It's about being able to see ourselves honestly, which is always the first step in speaking and living our truth "out loud" with others. A good way to think about this is that in life there are things that are "above the line" (actions we take, habits we have, roles we play, and so on), and there are things that are "below the line" (thoughts, feelings, attitudes, beliefs, values, imagination, and much more). Since we live in such an action-oriented, results-driven world, we focus most of our attention on what we do, the actions we take, the roles we play, or the habits we have (or think we should have)—all above-the-line stuff.

Action is important and essential, but the major part of our genuine success and fulfillment in life is created below the line, not above it. In other words, everything in the seen or physical world has to originate in the unseen or invisible world first. I can't take an action, make a goal happen, or even say anything without first thinking, having a belief, holding a specific attitude, and more. All of this below-the-line stuff makes up who we really are and not only informs our actions, words, and roles in life, it dictates them.

The more we're able to see and understand ourselves at the deepest (below the line) level, the more access we have to being free, open, and authentic in our relationships, work, and lives.

How to Know Ourselves More Deeply

Knowing ourselves is an evolutionary process, not a destination. There are, however, many things you can do that will give you a greater understanding and awareness of who you truly are. Here's a list of some important things you can do to know yourself more deeply.

1. Pay attention. Increase your awareness of yourself by paying close attention to the things you say and do, how you interact with others, what thoughts and feelings you have, and how you show up in life. The more conscious of yourself you can be, in a nonjudgmental way, the more you'll be able know and understand yourself. See if you can observe yourself and your life while you're living it. Being in the present moment and not constantly thinking about the past or worrying about the future will help you pay attention to yourself in a healthy way.

2. Learn about yourself and your personality. There are many great ways to learn more about yourself and your personality these days. Personality assessment tools such as Myers-Briggs, the DISC profile, Strengths Finder, the Enneagram, and many others are used all over the world for both business and personal purposes. These and other assessment tools are a great way for you to more fully understand some of your own unique qualities, traits, quirks, and tendencies.

3. Appreciate your strengths. Take inventory of what you do well, what gifts and talents you have, and the things you're proud of about yourself. This isn't about bragging or being arrogant, it's about being grateful for who you are, the positive qualities you have, and all that you bring to the people in your life and to life in general. Getting in touch with and being aware of your strengths is an important aspect of knowing who you truly are. In most cases, we each have many more gifts, talents, and strengths than we give ourselves credit for.

4. Have compassion for your weaknesses. See if you can be aware of your "weaknesses" and "shortcomings" in a compassionate way. Knowing what you're not so good at or can improve upon is important. However, remember that your Gremlin will often go to town on you in a very negative, critical, and judgmental way, especially if you're trying something new, whenever you get scared, or even if you want to make positive changes in your life. Being able to go easy on yourself, and reminding yourself that no one is perfect (and that's not the goal anyway) and that you were, are, and will always do the best you can in each and every moment of your life, can both give you access to more fully knowing yourself and give you a sense of peace and freedom from your own negative self-criticism.

5. Accept yourself. Self-acceptance is an essential aspect of knowing who you are. Without being a victim or overly dramatic, it's important to acknowledge some of the challenges that you've faced in the past and still face in your life today. You can appreciate yourself for overcoming and dealing with these challenges, and also be aware of as many of your strengths and weaknesses as possible—in a positive way. Accepting yourself is not about doing everything "right," ignoring or denying aspects of who you are, or being resigned in any way—it's about making peace with all of who you are, both light and dark. Acceptance eliminates suffering. This is a simple concept, but, as we all know, is not always easy to do. When you practice self-acceptance, you gain a deeper awareness and appreciation for who you are.

6. Get feedback. Allow people to give you honest feedback—family members, friends, co-workers, and others. Be open to what people have to say about you and ask them to be honest. This takes courage, but when you're willing to listen to the feedback of others, you can gain a deeper awareness and insight about who you are, how you show up in life, and how you affect others—both positively and negatively. The important thing to remember about other people's feedback is that none of it is "true" with a capital "T"—it's just their opinions. For many of us, myself included, this can be difficult to remember, especially if their feedback seems negative or critical to us. However, the more feedback you get, the more you'll be able to see and hear consistencies that can help you more fully know who you are. It's impossible for you to see yourself objectively or to see outside of your own personal experience, so the feedback of others can be invaluable—both positive acknowledgement and critical suggestions.

These are all things that you can do on a regular basis in your life to more fully and deeply know and understand yourself. Knowing yourself is the first and most important aspect of your journey toward deeper authenticity.

Looking Within

James is a friend of mine who has always had a good amount of outward success in his life. He comes from a wealthy family, did very well in school, and has a thriving business that he started himself and has built up over the past ten years. Although he'd had a number of romantic relationships with women over the years, he'd struggled to find "the one." For much of his life in his twenties and through the first part of his thirties, James always seemed to find women who in his opinion weren't quite satisfying. He'd usually end up cheating on them or would find other ways to sabotage the relationship once he got "bored."

A few years ago James and I had a conversation. We hadn't talked in a while and I asked him how things were going with his love life at the time. He said, "Well, I've been dating this woman named Stacy for a while—she's great and has all the qualities that I say are important to me. However, I still find myself getting bored and restless, like I always do. This time it finally hit me, maybe it has something to do with me and not all of the women that I date."

"You think?" I asked, somewhat sarcastically. I was actually happy to hear James say this. I appreciated his introspection and honesty.

He then said, "For the first time in my life I'm starting to think about this stuff and have even been reading some books on relationships and personal development. And, Stacy and I have hired a relationship coach and are doing sessions with her together and individually. I'm looking at aspects of my past, my relationship with my mom and women in general, how I feel about myself, and more. It's challenging, but eye-opening. I'm learning a lot about myself, my patterns, and some of my fears about women and relationships. I probably should've done this a long time ago."

Working with a coach, James started to tell the truth, get more real, and look at himself in a more authentic way. He was able to see that he was the common denominator in all of his relationships and that if he wanted to have a successful relationship with Stacy, he'd need to take a look within himself. He saw that his issues with Stacy and with women in general had a lot to do with his anger toward his mother—feeling as though she was never satisfied with him and that no matter what he did it was never enough. He was both projecting this lack of satisfaction onto the women he dated and protecting himself from potential pain and hurt down the road by pulling away as he always did.

Through his increased self-awareness, reading books, working with his coach, talking honestly to people in his life like me, and resolving some issues directly with both his mother and with Stacy, James was able to alter some of his relationship patterns in a significant way. He and Stacy recently got married, and their combined commitment to honesty, self-awareness, and growth are essential factors in the success of their relationship. While there is no guarantee that James and Stacy will stay together forever or that their relationship will be fulfilling for both of them, the chances are much greater for their ultimate happiness, given that they're willing to look within themselves, talk to each other honestly, and do some work together to have their marriage be what they want it to be.

 EXERCISE
Personal Inquiry

One of the greatest tools for knowing ourselves is the power of inquiry. Asking yourself questions and allowing yourself to stay in an ongoing inquiry is incredibly enlightening. I often end my individual or group coaching sessions by giving my clients a question or two to ponder between sessions. The goal is for them to sit with the questions and ask them to themselves over and over again, to see what comes up.

Following is a long list of powerful questions you can ask yourself now, later today, throughout the week, and in an ongoing way that will allow you to delve more deeply into who you really are. Feel free to use your journal or write down some thoughts now and in the future. Also, feel free to engage in conversations with the people in your life about these questions.

- What is most important to you in life?
- What are you grateful for?
- What are your core values?

- What motivates you in the most important areas of your life?
- What do you worry about most?
- What brings you joy?
- What are your priorities?
- What upsets you most?
- What is your vision for your life?
- What gifts do you have that you want to give to others and to the world?

Choosing to Grow

For us to really know ourselves and be ourselves in an authentic way, I believe we must consciously choose to grow as human beings. There are a lot of ways we can grow—physically, mentally, emotionally, and spiritually—and even more different methods we can use. The form of our growth is not as important as our intention for growing. It doesn't really matter if we do it through books, counseling, workshops, audios, religion, yoga, coaching, meditation, spirituality, classes, bodywork, prayer, metaphysics, videos, or any combination of these or other things. All of these can be great methods and catalysts for us to learn about ourselves, heal, change, and ultimately grow as human beings.

However, these "methods" are all above the line and are only as valuable as they speak to us, work for us, and produce the kind of growth and transformation we're seeking—all of which takes place below the line, deep within us. Too often we get hung up on the form of our growth, trying to find the "right" way to do it and then being self-righteous with others about our personal approach. As I have learned myself many times, this is a negative ego trap and really isn't that important. What's most important is our commitment to growing, which will continue to evolve throughout our lives, as will the various growth forms or methods we choose to use.

The deeper and more important questions for us to ask ourselves are

1. Why do I want to grow?
2. What's important for me to look at, deal with, heal, and transform about myself and my life?
3. How can I create the best possible circumstance in which my growth will be supported, enhanced, and fulfilled?

Why We Want to Grow

Looking at why we want to grow is important. For most of us, our initial desire to grow and change comes from circumstances or reactions that leave us feeling as though we're "bad" or that there's something really wrong with us that needs to be fixed. While this is a very common initial motivation, if it continues to be our sole reason for "growth," it's usually inauthentic and ineffective, because all we're trying to do is "fix" the things we think are broken, and as soon as we do that or make the assumption (for whatever reason) that we can't, we stop "growing." I personally spent many years, and from time to time still find myself, relating to my own growth as a series of neverending "issues" or "maladies" I'm simply trying to resolve, erroneously thinking that one day they'll all be "fixed" and then I'll be "done" growing.

Real growth, I believe, comes from a deep place within us that wants to heal, yes, but also yearns for a true sense of understanding, love, peace, awareness, joy, connection, gratitude, aliveness, fun, evolution, authenticity, and more—for ourselves, others, and our world. Our own personal motivation for growth is always unique, but it's important that we ask ourselves "why" and that we're both satisfied and inspired by our honest answer. If not, and our focus remains on fixing our problems, it's important that we recognize this as the ego trap that it is, and keep looking deeper.

Knowing What's Important for Us

Understanding what's most important for us to look at, heal, and transform is fundamental. This, like so many other aspects of our growth and development, will evolve over time. Being aware consciously of not only why we want to grow but what specifically we want to work on is essential. Usually the things we focus on when we begin to "grow"—losing weight, making money, healing a physical problem, finding a partner, getting over a loss of any kind, and so on, while important, are not the real issues or reasons, just the above-the-line circumstances. When we take a deeper look, below the line, at what underlies these initial reasons or circumstances, we can find the true nature of ourselves and our desire to grow. While there's nothing wrong with accomplishing goals, healing an injury or loss, making money, being fit and healthy, finding a great relationship, and more, what we're usually after is more about a deep sense of fulfillment, gratitude, and love—for ourselves, others, and life. This is where our real power comes from and how we can live a life of depth, realness, and meaning.

What someone does on the surface may look the same in terms of form—going to church or temple, taking a workshop, doing yoga, meditating, working with a healer or body worker, reading a book, hiring a coach, and so on. However, the underlying reason and focus will not only vary from person to person but have a dramatic impact on the effectiveness and outcome of the process. For example, there could be a hundred people attending a personal growth workshop, and not only will each of them be there for a different reason, what they choose to focus on and pay attention to will affect what they get out of the workshop, as much or more than the quality of the workshop itself.

Knowing the Best Methods for Our Growth

Seeking out the best possible circumstance and method for our own growth is vital. This can be challenging because we often have very specific ideas about what is and isn't "appropriate" based on how we were raised, our religious background, and our own opinions or our fears of the judgments of others. The key to finding people, methods, and situations that support your own personal growth is trusting yourself. Listen to your inner guidance, look for people that you resonate with, and know that if your intention and motivation are both strong and clear, the methods, people, and processes will show up in the right timing and the right form for you.

Whenever you're working with someone one-on-one, reading a book, taking a workshop, or doing anything else with the intention of growing, keep checking in with yourself—before, during, and, most important, afterward, to see how you feel and notice the impact of the specific method or process on you and your life. The goal is for each of us to be the author of our own life and growth by choosing how we grow and what methods work best for us consciously. Remember the paradox—it's not about the form, it's about the substance, experience, and outcome and at the same time using the best possible methods we can find will enhance our ability to grow.

EXERCISE
Your Own Personal Growth

In order for you to deepen your awareness of yourself and your own personal growth journey, take a few moments to answer the following questions as deeply and honestly as you can on a piece of paper or in your journal.

1. What is your current and honest motivation for "grow-ing"? (That is, why are you reading this book; why do you read books like this in general; what motivates you to take workshops, work with a coach or counselor, or do anything else that you consider aspects of your own personal growth?)
2. What is most important for you to look at, deal with, heal, and transform about yourself and your life right now?
3. How can you create the best possible circumstance in which your growth will be supported, enhanced, and fulfilled? In other words, what are the best methods and approaches you can take at this point in your life to support you in growing?

For this third question, it's a good idea to think about and take inventory of what you've done in the past and what has worked for you, as well as what you're currently drawn to or interested in as it relates to your own personal growth and development (both specific methods and your desired outcomes).

My Own Growth Journey

I've always been interested in people, my own process, and the genuine thoughts and feelings of others and myself. From the time I was a kid, the two things that I've been most interested in—in myself, others, and life—are passion and pain. What I'm passionate about and what creates pain in my life—as well as what others are passionate or

in pain about—have always been to me the most interesting aspects of life. As much as I like to talk about sports,
politics, business, entertainment, and other stuff that does
genuinely interest me, these things pale in comparison to
what I consider the "real stuff" of life.

Even with this interest as a child and adolescent, I was
never quite able to understand or articulate my deep desire
to "grow" (although I don't think I would have referred to
it that way as a kid). However, looking back, I see that it
was always central to my life. Everything I did was in order
to seek passion or confront pain, and I was constantly curious about other people's passion and pain as well. My
enthusiasm for people, sports, and life dictated a lot of
what I did and said as a child and adolescent. And, with my
parent's divorce, my dad's bipolar disorder, our financial
difficulties as a family, and some of the other challenges
of my childhood, coupled with my deep sense of fear and
insecurity, there was a lot of pain in my life growing up.
When I was twenty years old, my junior year in college,
life took a significant and dramatic turn for me personally,
and my journey of conscious growth began.

It all started on New Year's Eve 1994. I jumped in the
middle of a fight that my friends had gotten into—partly to
prove I was "tough" and partly to see if I could help break
it up. Not being much of a fighter myself and having had
a few too many drinks that night, not only was I unsuccessful at being tough or breaking up the fight, I ended
up getting punched badly and sustained what is known
as a "blow out" fracture to my right eye. As soon as it

happened, I couldn't see straight. Over the next few days and weeks I struggled with double vision and saw a number of doctors and specialists who considered operating on my eye to correct the problem. All of this happened right before the beginning of the baseball season at Stanford that year—a very important year for me, as I was hoping to play well and get drafted by a pro team that June.

The physical injury was very upsetting and scary to me. The deeper pain I experienced, however, was mental, emotional, and, as I ultimately would come to realize, spiritual. It rattled me in a way I'd never experienced. I didn't know what was wrong with me. I'd never felt so awful in my entire life. I obsessed about my eye injury, but even more found that I was thinking and feeling some of the darkest, most negative thoughts and feelings about myself I'd ever had. Even though looking back on it now it seems somewhat irrational, I felt as though I had damaged my life in such a profound way and for a stupid reason (an alcohol-induced, mindless fight that I didn't even want to be in to begin with). I hated myself for it. I felt embarrassed and flawed. Everywhere I looked in my life seemed so bleak, painful, and negative.

Why was I so miserable? I had to find out, to understand myself, to know who I really was and why this had happened.

According to the psychiatrist at the student health center, I was clinically depressed. I started to see her regularly and to take Prozac, the anti-depression medication she prescribed for me. I was well aware of depression and its potentially devastating implications from all of my experience with my father and his manic-depression. Growing up, I was convinced that I would never get depressed, although secretly terrified that I too had the "family curse" of mental illness that my father and many other members of my family suffered from. When it happened to me, I thought my life was over. I was in so much pain, I couldn't see a way out of it and even began to have serious thoughts of killing myself. Although up to that point in my life death was something that terrified me more than almost anything, the thought of living my life in so much mental and emotional pain seemed way worse than whatever fears I had about what death might be like.

The counseling I got from the student health center and the medication I was taking were supposed to address and alleviate the symptoms of my depression, but they didn't seem to work in any genuine way. Something deep within me, even at that time, knew that what was going on within me was much more than about my eye injury or even the painful episode of depression I was experiencing. While I did want the pain to stop, I also knew I wanted to go deeper into it and understand where it was coming from and why I was experiencing it—not just get rid of it. I'm not sure I was fully aware of it at the time, but I was ready to grow and wanted to look more deeply at myself, my life, and the nature of life itself.

Thankfully, I was introduced to an incredible man and counselor named Chris Andersonn. Chris isn't a traditional psychologist; he's more of a spiritual counselor, guide, and teacher. The first time we spoke on the phone, which is how we did our counseling sessions, I remember sobbing deeply—as an expression of my pain, but also with a sense of liberation. Chris said to me, "I feel a great deal of fear and sadness within you." Then he asked, "Are you feeling a lot of pressure and expectation, in general and specifically from your mother?" He said all of this without really knowing much about me, my past, or the specific circumstances I was dealing with. For one of the first times in my entire life, I felt seen, heard, and understood—both by what Chris said and by the awareness and emotional understanding he had about me and what I was going through. I immediately trusted him and knew he was someone important in my life who was here to teach me and help me heal and grow.

Chris and I began to work together, and he taught me many important things about myself and my life that I'd never known consciously but had always been drawn to at a deep level. He helped me see how much anger, shame, and fear I was carrying around with me—related to my father's illness, my mother's desire for me to succeed, how I was raised, my body image, the intense pressure I felt about playing baseball, and much more. More important, I began to see how these emotions were affecting my life in a negative way and that more than any of the specific circumstances it was the emotions coupled with my lack of self-love, forgiveness, and appreciation that were causing me so much pain.

He taught me how to meditate and introduced me to metaphysical and spiritual healing techniques for releasing these intense emotions—acknowledging them through writing, speaking, visualizing, meditating, and actually feeling them fully. I also learned from Chris that my beliefs—along with my thoughts, feelings, attitudes, choices, and decisions—create my reality, and that helped me see why and how I'd actually created both the pain and the success in my life at that time, as well as in the past, and of course as I moved forward.

In the process of our work together, Chris literally saved my life. It took a number of months of intense sessions with him and others before I was able to see the light at the end of the tunnel and come out of my depression. My eye injury healed, but more important, I began to heal and open up at a much deeper level.

As scary, difficult, and painful as that time in my life was, it was also incredibly enlightening. Looking back on it now, I can see that the injury to my eye and my subsequent depression were the above-the-line circumstances that woke me up to my deeper desire for growth. More than fourteen years later, I continue to work with Chris, and I've been introduced to many other wonderful teachers, coaches, mentors, healers, workshops, books, techniques, spiritual practices, and more. My own desire to grow, heal, learn, and evolve became and continues to be the central theme of my life, my work, and my relationships to others—especially to my wife Michelle and our two daughters.

For us to become more of who we really are, to live with authenticity, to wake up and create the life we want to live consciously, and to be able to experience true joy and peace in life, it's necessary for us to know ourselves at the deepest level and continue this personal exploration for our entire lives. Even though this process is not always easy or convenient, as we do this we can grow and evolve as human beings—not by accident, but by choice!

The Importance of Guidance

Having good guidance is an essential aspect of us knowing ourselves and being able to grow. Another interesting paradox of life, however, is that all growth takes place within us and comes from us, yet at the same time it's difficult for us to grow without the support and feedback of others. No matter how aware we are, how gifted we may be in a specific area, or how much we've learned in our lives, we can all use constant guidance if we are to continue to evolve and grow. Even elite athletes need to have coaching and feedback in order to stay on top of their game and continue to expand. The same is true for all of us in life. Being authentic and living in a way that is true to ourselves is, at some level, about us and only us. However, the feedback of other people whom we trust and respect, and who have wisdom and perspective to share with us, can be an invaluable part of our growth process and our journey of life.

While it's important for us to seek out guidance if we're to grow and evolve as human beings, at the same time, we need to be a bit selective about whom we allow to guide us on our journey. I do believe we can learn from anyone and that each person we encounter on our path has something important to teach us, if we pay attention. For us to truly grow in a healthy way, however, we must choose our guides, mentors, coaches, and teachers deliberately.

As the saying goes, "there's only one light, but many lamps." With more and more books like this being written all the time, new workshops to take, lots and lots of people wanting to coach us these days—many of whom claim to have the ultimate "secret" to living a life of happiness, health, wealth, and love—it's up to us to decide whom we pay attention to and to notice what resonates with us most profoundly. The best way to approach this is to be as open as possible, to look for the "good stuff" in what everyone has to say and teach, but to be very clear about where we are, what we want and need, and what works best for us.

Knowing ourselves and growing aren't about things always feeling good or comfortable to us. In fact, some of the best and most important growth opportunities and feedback that we'll get in our lives may not feel good initially but sometimes will be exactly what we need to do or hear at a particular time in our lives in order to go to the next level of our evolution. The goal is to trust ourselves, listen to our inner guidance, and remember that we are always in charge of our life and our growth. Real growth is not about achievement, it's about evolution—going deeper within ourselves, discovering more about who we are, and creating a real sense of authenticity and depth.

Out of Our Comfort Zones

Lisa hired me to coach her to work on some communication issues she was facing at work with clients and with her boss. Within a short time, on the basis of some good work done by Lisa and some coaching from me about listening, being present, and speaking from her heart, she was beginning to improve her communication at work and she was pleased with the results.

As often is the case with many of my coaching clients, once we addressed her initial concerns and goals, which are usually pretty simple and straightforward, as was true for Lisa, we began to delve into other important aspects of her life—more personal, below-the-line stuff. She was struggling with some difficult issues in her relationships with her husband Jim and her elderly parents, and with some deep, life-long insecurities about her value in her career and as a woman who'd chosen not to have children.

Over the next two years, Lisa and I had regular sessions every week or every other week. We worked a lot on her taking responsibility for her reactions, thoughts, and feelings (that is, on not being a "victim"), among other things. She began to speak up more with Jim, tell her parents what she was really thinking and feeling, take more risks, and ask for more responsibility at work. With as much compassion and honesty as possible, I pushed and challenged Lisa a lot to step outside of her comfort zone. Although at times she resisted, argued, and even failed, overall her progress was wonderful.

She and Jim began to talk more, spend more time together, and have regular dates and romantic getaways— something she really wanted. She created some important boundaries with her parents and shared some things with them she'd been afraid to say for most of her life, which gave her a sense of peace and freedom she didn't know was possible and was so grateful for, especially given their age and health condition. She even got a new job making a lot more money and with a significant amount of responsibility—something she'd previously been convinced she couldn't do. More important than any of these specific results and outcomes in Lisa's life, she began to trust herself, make peace with herself, and appreciate herself in a genuine way.

All of these positive changes took place in Lisa's life because she was ready to grow. She was also open to the feedback, coaching, and guidance that she got from me in our sessions and from others through books, workshops, her church, and elsewhere. As the saying goes, "when the student is ready, the teacher will appear." This was true for Lisa and is true for all of us when we remember that our growth comes from within us, always, and, paradoxically, we can't grow without the feedback and guidance of others.

PRACTICES

This book, and any other book you read in the future, can have the biggest impact on you if you take any information and inspiration you get from reading it and put it into action in your daily life.

Following are a number of simple practices that you can use. Most of them can be done alone, but some require other people or resources. All of them are designed to increase your level of self-awareness and to practice this very important principle of *knowing yourself*. And there are clearly many more practices and techniques that you can use. The idea of this list is to get you thinking and also to get you into action. My challenge to you is to pick a few of these practices that either resonate with you or scare you (either of which, as you know, are signs that something important is happening) and start doing them as soon as possible. Have fun and remember they're "practices," so you don't have to get them "right" and you can't really mess them up.

1. Create a daily self-awareness practice. Do something each day that causes you to stop, quiet your mind, check in with yourself, and feel your feelings. This may be meditation, prayer, a time of quiet reflection or inquiry in the shower or the car, a walk, or anything else. The form is not as important as the intention. The goal is to give yourself some time and space once a day, or more, to be aware of yourself fully—physically, mentally, and emotionally—and to notice and feel what's truly going on within you, below the line.

2. Journal regularly. This is a very powerful and simple practice that can have life-altering results. As often as you can, take time to write down your honest thoughts and feelings in your journal. Get yourself a nice journal, one that feels good to look at, touch, and write in. It can also be on your computer, or in the form of a personal blog. Whatever way, create a safe and sacred place for you to express your honest thoughts and feelings about yourself, your process, and your life in writing. It doesn't matter what you write, how long you write, how it looks, or even what it says. The key is for it to be real and for you to be able to express what and how you're feeling—fear, love, sadness, excitement, anger, joy, confusion, gratitude, guilt, enthusiasm, and so much more. Don't judge yourself, just express yourself and do it as often as you can.

3. Take a personality assessment. The personality assessment tools I mentioned earlier in this chapter—Myers-Briggs, the DISC Profile, Strengths Finder, and the Enneagram, among others—can be wonderful ways for you to gain more awareness of yourself and to understand more about who you are. Of all of them, I recommend the Enneagram the most—it has been around for more than four thousand years and contains a great amount of wisdom and depth. Do some research and find one that fits best for you. Most of them are simple, easy, and inexpensive (if not free) to get. If you've taken one or more of these assessment tests in the past, look or think back to your results and see what you gained or can gain from that feedback about yourself in the context of our discussion here in this book about authenticity. And consider retaking the test or finding another one—just as with rereading a good book, you often get new things out of it the second or third time around.

4. Work with a coach or counselor. One-on-one work with a coach or a counselor is not for everyone but can often become an essential aspect of your growth and awareness. Choose who you work with consciously—make sure you trust them, you feel good about them, and something in your gut tells you that this person has important things to teach you. Remember the paradox, that knowing who you are, growing, and everything you need is already within you . . . and at the same time you can't know yourself or grow as effectively or quickly without the feedback and guidance of others. If you've worked with lots of coaches and counselors in the past or are working with one or more now, check in with yourself to make sure you're getting what you want from this person and your work with them. If you're not working with someone right now or have never worked with anyone in this way, notice what's stopping you from doing so and see if you want or need to move beyond that to find someone to work with. Having a coach or counselor you trust, who pushes you, who calls you out with love and honesty, and who you can lean on is invaluable in your journey toward deeper awareness and authenticity.

5. Take personal development workshops. Whether you're someone, like me, who takes workshops all the time, or you've never taken a personal development course in your entire life, workshops can be another essential aspect of learning, growth, and awareness. There are so many options these days—which is both wonderful and challenging.

Take some inventory of what's important to you, ask people you trust, and see what resonates with you most, then sign yourself up for a personal development workshop and make it a habit to take courses as often as you're able and interested. This investment in yourself is one of the best things you can do for your life and your growth. In the Resources section of this book, I list a number of great workshops and seminars that I highly recommend. Check out that list and others and find some workshops for yourself.

This first principle, Know Yourself, in and of itself can transform your life. When we know who we are at the deepest level, we have the ability to make peace with ourselves and live with a deeper sense of authenticity in our work, our relationships, and our lives.

Now that we've looked at the importance of self-awareness (Principle 1), we can take the next essential step in our journey toward greater authenticity: transforming our fear (Principle 2).

4

PRINCIPLE 2

transform your fear

"It takes courage to grow up and become who you really are."

—*e. e. cummings*

Fear is something that we all experience throughout our lives, especially on our journey toward deeper authenticity. Being who we really are, expressing ourselves honestly, being bold, and going for what we want in life can cause a great deal of fear in us. As we discussed in Chapter Two, our fears about failure, success, rejection, disappointment, judgment and more often have an impact on our ability to be ourselves and in many cases can stop us from speaking up and going for what we really want in an authentic way.

115

Many of us run away or hide from our fears because they seem scary, uncomfortable, or embarrassing. However, most things that mean a lot to us in life don't show up without any fear at all. And as we strive to live with authenticity, it's inevitable that we'll encounter quite a bit of fear along our path.

Most of us erroneously think that as we evolve in life our goal should be to get rid of fear. Unfortunately, completely ridding ourselves of fear isn't possible or even desirable. Fear is an essential part of growth and can be used in a positive way for authenticity and fulfillment—if we're willing to deal with it in a direct, honest, and conscious way. However, the bigger problem with fear isn't usually the fear itself, but our resistance to or denial of it.

This second principle, Transform Your Fear, is all about understanding our fear—knowing it, appreciating it, admitting it, owning it, embracing it, and ultimately using it as a tool on our path toward greater authenticity. The question isn't whether or not we experience fear in our lives (because we all do and always will for as long as we live); the more important question for each of us to ask and answer is, How can I move through my fears in an honest way so they don't stop me from being who I really am and going for what I truly want in life?

Making Peace with Fear

Since fear is unavoidable in life, our goal is to make peace with fear and to stop resisting or running away from it.

As Carl Jung famously said, "What you resist persists." This is true in every aspect of life and particularly as it relates to our fear. It takes a lot of energy, as you and I know, to go around in life fighting against our fear or pretending we don't have any, when of course we do. The better we understand fear in general and, more specifically, the more aware we are of our own fears, the more power we have in dealing with and ultimately moving beyond them.

Understanding Fear

Our first step in making peace with fear is understanding it. According to Dictionary.com, some of the definitions of fear are

- A distressing emotion aroused by impending danger, evil, pain, and so on, whether the threat is real or imagined; the feeling or condition of being afraid.
- A specific instance of or propensity for such a feeling: *an abnormal fear of heights.*
- Concern or anxiety; solicitude: *a fear for someone's safety.*
- That which causes a feeling of being afraid; that of which a person is afraid: *Cancer is a common fear.*

Although these and other definitions all explain the concept of fear, as we all know, it's much more than a concept. Fear is an intense emotion that also carries with it a physical aspect. It triggers the familiar "fight or flight" response in our bodies, characterized by increased heart rate, breathing, muscle tension, and more, which can pump us up to escape from danger or defend ourselves against a predator. This initial physiological response is followed by a slower, more detailed psychological assessment and emotional experience, during which we become conscious of feeling afraid—thinking fearful thoughts, worrying, feeling scared, or sometimes pretending we aren't afraid when really we are.

Beyond a normal fight or flight response, we often have emotional fears that occur when we think about or begin to take an authentic action of any kind—say, do, or go for something we truly want—a dream, goal, job, relationship, and so on. Whenever we sense danger or confrontation, whether real or imaginary, a gland situated on our kidneys releases a mixture of chemicals commonly known as adrenaline. Ironically, our bodies have similar physical reactions to both fear and excitement.

Everyone Gets Scared

As a kid I remember how scared I would get walking up to home plate when it was my turn to bat in Little League baseball games. My legs would shake, my heart would pound, and my throat would feel dry. Sometimes it was even hard for me to breathe. I worried about striking out, letting my teammates down, looking foolish, getting hit by the ball, and more. I figured I was so scared because I was young, and that once I got older and stronger my fears would go away. Although my fears did change as I got older; even though I loved playing baseball and was good at it, in every game I ever played in—whether I was hitting, pitching, or in the field—I experienced an element of fear (sometimes quite intense). I know now that everyone else on the field was feeling their own version of that same fear—I just couldn't feel it and see it in them the way I felt it within myself. A lot of the guys I played ball with as a kid and as I got older, like me, did a great job of faking it and pretending they weren't scared. This is what most of us do in life.

Everyone gets scared. Many of us are walking around in a constant state of anxiety. We've just gotten used to living in fear and don't really notice it. It's like when you sit in a quiet room with the air conditioner on—after a while you don't hear it anymore and think that it's totally silent, until it goes off and gets really quiet. Then you realize how loud the air conditioner actually was.

Instead of allowing ourselves to feel and experience our fear, we judge the fears we have, think we shouldn't have them, or try to deny them altogether. It's not socially acceptable to be scared in many situations, and most of us aren't that comfortable admitting to others that we're scared. Can you imagine if a politician, media personality, or celebrity came on TV or did an interview in which they told us all how scared they were about being there or doing what they do? In our own lives, it would be very odd if we met with our boss, talked to someone at the bank, or had a conversation at a party with friends and shared with them some of our honest fears and doubts. It's not that this never happens; it's just not all that common and isn't normally done in an authentic way.

Our denial of fear often has us in turn do some pretty unhealthy things (drink too much, overeat, control others, worry, lie, avoid all kinds of things, overwork, judge people, and more), all in an attempt to pretend we aren't scared when we really are.

I gave a keynote speech at an event for one of my corporate clients—a big international bank. At the end of my presentation, Frank, one of the leaders within the group, came up to talk to me. He looked around a few times before he shook my hand and then he leaned over and said to me in somewhat of a hushed voice, "You know, I get scared all the time and worry that I'll mess things up, blow big deals, or let people down. Given my position here, my age and experience, and the amount of success and responsibility I have, I don't really feel like I can admit it when I feel scared. I appreciated your talk today. You helped me realize that there's nothing wrong with me for feeling like this. Thank you."

I was grateful for Frank's honesty and feedback. I could tell by the look in his eye and the tone of his voice that not only was he telling the truth, but that something shifted in him by being able to tell me about it. Like Frank, many of us don't feel as though we can admit our fear and insecurity, or if we do, we worry that people will think badly of us or no longer respect who we are. We have a tendency to take ourselves very seriously, have you noticed?

However, when we realize and accept that being afraid is one of the most basic and natural human emotions, and that no matter how confident, peaceful, or successful a person is, everyone experiences fear, we can actually begin to make peace not only with our fears but with ourselves. People who achieve great things in life and, more important, who are able to create a true sense of fulfillment for themselves aren't devoid of fear—they're simply more able and willing to be honest about their fears and thus can move through them with a sense of ease and grace. Understanding the universal nature of fear is essential in our ability to be authentic.

Know Your Fear

The saying "no fear" became popular about ten or fifteen years ago thanks in part to the line of clothing with that saying on it and to people's increased interest and participation in extreme sports such as skydiving, bungee jumping, rock climbing, and so on.

I myself had a few "no fear" t-shirts that I wore proudly. While I appreciate the sentiment and the idea of getting past our fear and just going for it, what we actually want to do is know our fear (not deny it), so that we can learn from it and ultimately move through it in a conscious and positive way.

The more we know our fears and become intimately acquainted with what they are, how they feel, and what it looks like when we get scared, the easier it is for us to move through fear effectively when it inevitably shows up.

We want to create a healthy relationship with our fear. The analogy I often use with my clients is that of a "scary monster." We've spent most of our lives, in a figurative sense, running away from that monster and hiding inside our houses—boarding up the windows, turning off the lights, and hiding under the bed. Even though it may seem counterintuitive in many ways, opening the door, looking the monster in the eye, and inviting it into our house is how we can ultimately liberate ourselves from fear.

I get scared all the time—even doing the things I love most to do in my life—writing, coaching, leading workshops, and speaking. Sometimes when I walk up on stage to give a talk, especially to a large group of people, my legs and hands will shake because I'm so nervous. However, whenever I find that I'm experiencing intense fear like this, I try to know and understand this fear better, and ask myself, "What am I really afraid of?"

We're almost never afraid of what we're actually doing or even sometimes of what we think we're afraid of on the surface. I'm not usually all that scared about speaking in front of a large group of people—I do it all the time and really love it. What I'm most often scared of in those instances are people's judgments, my own perceived weaknesses and insecurities, looking like an idiot, or other self-imposed "threats" that in most cases aren't actually real, just imagined in my own mind. Because these are fears I'm familiar with, I've trained myself to not let them get in my way—even when I feel them intensely. My body still reacts to the adrenalin and I still feel the fear in my body, but that doesn't stop me from getting up and speaking anyway.

When we know and understand our fears and are willing to face them in an honest way, they don't have to hold us back from being our authentic selves and doing what we need and want to do.

Appreciating Our Fear

Appreciating our fear might seem like an odd thing to do, but it's very important. We experience fear for a reason, and it almost always has something valuable to teach us, if we pay attention to it. Fear can be a powerful motivator and teacher. And while we don't want to live our lives in a constant state of fear, being able to appreciate our fears will allow us to learn from them, make peace with them, and ultimately tap into them in a positive way. Think of some of the positive aspects of having fear. Fear can

- Save our lives and keep us from harm
- Let us know when something is important to us
- Teach us a lot about life, ourselves, and being human
- Give us access and insight into our vulnerability
- Show us places where we can grow and have more compassion for ourselves and others
- Connect us with other people in a profound, authentic, and universal way
- Give us opportunities to take risks and be courageous

These are some of the many things we can appreciate about our fear. Something I believe that's important for each of us to have as we continue to grow and evolve is a healthy sense of our fear. This not only means that we can sense "danger" in an effective way but also means that we're able to recognize fear as the natural response that it is. For example, one of my clients was a woman named Sue. When I met Sue, she was in her mid-forties and had worked in the technology industry in Silicon Valley for almost twenty-five years, ever since she graduated from college. She'd reached a professional crossroads in her life. She no longer enjoyed her job; the only part she really liked about what she did was mentoring, coaching, and working with the people on her team. Because of this, she decided to change directions completely. She wanted to become a life and business coach, as well as write books and lead workshops. She kept her day job at her technology company, but put herself in a coaching training program and decided to hire a coach, which turned out to be me.

After we'd been working together for a few months and Sue had encountered some challenges in her initial attempts to get her new coaching business started, she said to me, "I don't understand why I'm so nervous about doing this. I've been a part of startup companies before, and I love coaching the people on my team, but for some reason the thought of going out on my own terrifies me."

My response to her was, "Good! That means this really matters to you and it's wonderful that you're in touch with, aware of, and willing to admit your fear about it. Now, here's where the real fun and the real work begin. First of all, have some compassion for yourself and remember that fear is a normal human emotion—especially when you're doing something new like this. Second, between now and our next session, ask yourself honestly, 'Why am I so scared? What specifically am I afraid of? And, how can this fear help me as I create my new career?'"

In our next coaching session Sue said, "I've been giving myself some time and space to really think about and more importantly feel some of my deepest fears about starting my new business as a coach. I realize that many of my surface-level fears about making enough money, what people will think about me for leaving my successful career and starting a new one, and others like that, while true, aren't what's really holding me back. My deeper fears are that I won't be any good at this, that I might not be able to help people or even worse might do them harm, and that if I try to do this and fail, everyone will know and see, especially me, that I'm a total fraud." When Sue shared this last fear, her voice quivered and she began to cry. I felt the honesty and vulnerability of what she shared and appreciated it.

I said, "Sue, thanks for being real and telling the truth. Good work! It takes courage to be honest with yourself like this and to admit it to someone else. I acknowledge you for your vulnerability." Then I asked, "How can these fears actually help you in this process?"

"I'm not exactly sure," she said. "I got a little stuck with that one. But as I thought about it, and based on some of what we've been talking about for the past few months, maybe these are similar fears to ones that some of my clients will be dealing with, and my own ability to work with them in my life will give me more compassion, awareness, and understanding for them."

Sue was exactly right. Over the next few months we worked a lot on her accepting her fears, sharing them with others, and allowing herself to feel them by talking about them honestly, writing them down, and spending time on walks and in meditations actually feeling them. It wasn't about her dwelling on her fear or obsessing about her worries, it was about her allowing herself to experience them, learn from them, and ultimately appreciate them and use them for her own growth. While Sue did not "rid" herself of these fears completely, which is never really the goal anyway, she was able to move through them and integrate them into her life by simply allowing herself to feel and express them in an authentic way. By doing this not only was she able to make peace with her fears and with herself, she was able to find the courage to leave her technology job and become a full-time life and business coach who inspires people in an authentic and profound way.

EXERCISE
Knowing and Appreciating Your Fear

Part 1

Think about or write down something important that you've wanted to do or say for a while, but haven't done so because fear stopped you. It could be something "big" or "small" (a conversation; a change in career, relationship, or living situation; a purchase; having a child; letting something go; or anything else).

Part 2

Think about or write down your honest fears about doing or saying this specific thing. Go deep and really allow yourself to think about and feel what you're afraid of as it relates to this.

Part 3

Think about or write down some things you can appreciate about these specific fears. How can getting in touch with these fears help you make peace with them and even give you the courage or motivation to do or say this exact thing that has been scaring you?

Utilizing the Power of Our Fear in a Positive Way

When we're able to understand our fear, to remember that everyone gets scared and that there's nothing wrong with us when we do, to know what our fear looks like and feels like, and to appreciate it—even if it's uncomfortable—then we can tap into the power of our fear in a positive way. I realize that this is not the conventional way most of us approach fear, and some may argue that there's nothing positive about fear at all. However, when we look a bit deeper and are willing to be more honest, we can learn to transform our fear and actually utilize our fears in a very positive way—to be more free, authentic, and bold in our lives.

Not Allowing Our Fears to Stop Us

In the summer of 2004 my relationship with Michelle had come to a bit of a crossroads. We'd been together at that point for three-and-a-half years and had been living together for more than two years. A point of contention in our relationship, mostly from Michelle toward me (as well as from many of our friends, especially Michelle's close female friends) had to do with our future (that is, when and if we were going to get married).

We'd talked about this issue quite a bit—openly, honestly, and at times with some real intensity. We both did a pretty good job of listening to one another and being as compassionate with each other as we could. But in our lower moments it would get sticky, painful, and sometimes even ugly. Michelle would start to push and I would start to pull away—a very classic, stereotypical male-female dynamic in relationships, particularly related to commitment.

I knew deep within myself that if I chose to marry Michelle because I felt pressured by her or by our friends, or even because "it was time, we had been together long enough, and we were at the right age," I'd resent myself as well as her, and it wouldn't work. And while I was aware of some of my own fears and doubts about the idea of getting married—to Michelle and in general, I hadn't really looked at some of the deeper fears I had related to our relationship and to me as a potential husband and father.

Thanks to some great coaching, feedback, and counseling that I got at that time, I came face to face with some of

the deeper fears within me that I hadn't been aware of up
to that point in my life. The issue of trust, or lack of trust
more specifically, kept coming up for me. Deeper than
this, I realized for the first time in my life that I didn't trust
myself and I was actually scared of myself. Regarding being
with Michelle and the idea of getting married and creating
a family together, I didn't trust myself and my ability to do
that successfully.

I was scared I would ruin our relationship, her life,
and the lives of the kids we might have. I thought to
myself, "What if I fail, cheat on her, hurt her, hurt our kids,
get depressed, lose interest, don't have what it takes, end
up being a total loser as a husband and father, or die?" All
of these things seemed horrible. I realized I was avoiding
them unconsciously or trying to make sure they wouldn't
happen before I felt "ready" to get married.

Realizing this was quite painful, scary, and humbling
at first—but ultimately liberating. I knew that running
from these fears or pretending they didn't exist wouldn't
work—it was about admitting them, owning them, feeling them, expressing them, and transforming them. As
vulnerable and scared as I felt to admit these things, I sat
down with Michelle and shared them all with her. Michelle
wasn't upset with me; in fact she was grateful that I realized this and was willing to share it with her so honestly.
We had a series of wonderfully authentic and heartfelt conversations about our relationship, the future, and the fears
that we both had.

In realizing and sharing these things with Michelle I began to make peace with myself and the deeper fears I had about the possibility of Michelle and me getting married. I then asked myself an important question—"If I trusted myself fully, what would I do?" The answer was clear and obvious to me. Three weeks later, on August 1, 2004, I proposed to Michelle. The following June, we got married!

It's not that my fear about getting married and being a father magically vanished; believe me it didn't. I was, however, able to move through my fears to recognize them, own them, and express them—both to myself and to Michelle.

Since we got engaged in 2004 and married in 2005, I've still had many moments of fear and doubt—specifically related to being a husband to Michelle and a father to our two young girls, Samantha and Annarose. I often wonder, "Am I doing this right?" "What happens if I fail?" "Do they love me?" "Why did I say I would do this in the first place?" "This is hard, I want to run away," and more. When these fears come up, I do the best I can to face them directly, to be responsible for them, and to move through them honestly. I love being married to Michelle and having my girls—even when it gets difficult and scary. Being able to be honest with myself and with Michelle about my fears in a vulnerable and authentic way allows me to move through them so they don't have to stop me from loving her or our girls, or doing everything I can to be the best husband and father I know how to be.

CHECK THIS OUT
The Impact of Not Expressing Our Fear

According to Dr. Charles L. Whitfield, M.D., a physician, psychologist, author, and pioneer in trauma recovery, as well as a professor at Rutgers University's Institute on Alcohol and Drug Studies and a consultant research collaborator at the Center for Disease Control (CDC), "Unexpressed fear can result in anxiety disorders, insomnia, heart arrhythmias, sexual dysfunction and other stress-related illnesses."

How to Move Through Our Fear in a Positive Way

There are some simple but effective things we can do in order to transform our fear. Fear is a powerful emotion that can be channeled, transformed, and utilized in a positive way—if and when we're willing to face it and move through it consciously. Being able to transform our fear takes awareness, commitment, courage, and practice. For most of us, it's not easy. But as we become better at doing so, our ability to be free and authentic increases dramatically.

You can use the specific ideas listed here any time you're feeling a moderate or intense level of fear—about something specific or just in general. Going through these stages will allow you to make peace with your fear and ultimately support you in tapping into the power of your fear in a manner that reinforces your authenticity.

1. Admit your fear. Acknowledge your fear, tell the truth about it, and be real. When we feel scared and are willing to just admit it to ourselves with compassion, it often can take the edge off and give us a little breathing room. For example, if you're about to have an important conversation, give a presentation, meet someone new, take a risk, have a critical meeting, or do anything else that may cause you to be scared—it's always best to be real about your fear instead of pretending you aren't scared, talking yourself out of it, or just "grinning and bearing it." Admitting your fear is like taking the lid off of a pot of boiling water; it lets some of the steam out and takes off the pressure—even if it's just a little bit. Remember, everyone gets scared, there's nothing wrong with you for feeling fear, and the first and most important thing for you to do when fear shows up is to admit it.

2. Own your fear. This is about taking responsibility for your fear and owning it as yours, not anyone else's. In other words, not blaming anyone else or the situation for you feeling scared. We often think or say things like, "She makes me nervous." The truth is that we get nervous around her or have fear because of something we think she might do or say. This is not about semantics; it's a total shift in how we relate to life, others, circumstances, and our emotions—in this case our fear. We all have fear within us, and certain people or circumstances may cause us to get nervous. However, instead of blaming the thing or person, we can take responsibility for our own fear, since it's ours to begin with. Fully owning your fear is an essential aspect in your process of moving through it, transforming it, and using it in a positive way.

3. Feel your fear. For many of us, like me, talking about feeling our fear is often easier than actually feeling it. But before we can express our fear and transform it, we have to really feel it first. How do you do that? Notice it in your body—you may feel your heart beating, your hands getting clammy, your breath becoming short and shallow, or your legs shaking a bit. Think about it in your mind—you may have scary thoughts, be worried about lots of "worst-case scenarios," or find yourself fixated on all of the things you think will go wrong. Feel it emotionally—you can close your eyes and tap into your emotional state, and you may notice that you want to laugh, cry, yell, or something else. Whatever comes up physically, mentally, or emotionally—see if you can just be with it and allow yourself to really feel it.

4. Express your fear. Once you've felt your fear, there are many healthy ways you can express it. Speaking out loud to someone you trust, writing down your fears on a piece of paper, yelling loudly at the top of your lungs to let it out (assuming you're in a place where that's possible)—there are many ways you can express your fear as a way of allowing it to flow through you. For example, I'll often speak my fears out loud to Michelle on the phone before I go into important meetings, do a media interview, get up to give a speech, or do anything else that brings up fear within me. This always makes me feel better and helps me release and transform my fear. Michelle will sometimes ask me to do a nice loud Tarzan yell in my car or hotel room as a way of both expressing my fear and also changing my physical, mental, and emotional state—something that is also helpful in the process of expressing and moving through your fear. And if she thinks I need to relax even more and stop taking myself so seriously, which I have a tendency to do sometimes—she'll ask me to yodel a few times, until I crack up laughing (which is hard not to do when I hear myself try to yodel). Authentic laughter is often a great release and also a sign that we have expressed our fear in a way that has created some mental and emotional space.

5. Let go of your fear. This is another one that's often easier said than done for me and most of us. But letting go of your fear is important, powerful, and totally possible. We all have lots of experience with letting go of fears—we do it all the time in our lives, we just don't pay as much attention to the fears we let go of, we focus more of our attention on the ones we hang onto. Letting go of your fear is ultimately a choice. It's much easier and more natural to do once you've taken the time to admit, own, feel, and express your fears—however, it's always best when it's done intentionally. I'll say to myself (or even out loud), "I'm choosing to let go of my fear and to use its energy in a positive direction." This statement, or something similar to it, lets me know that I'm ready to let go. In order for this to work, your choice and declaration about letting go of your fear must be genuine, even if they start off feeling as though you're "faking it." And, paradoxically, it doesn't mean that just because you think about it or say you're letting it go, your fear will vanish completely. It's a process and a practice—the more you do this, the easier it gets.

6. Visualize the positive outcomes you desire. This is where you begin to transform the energy of your fear into something you can use in a positive way. By going through the other five stages, you're able to admit, own, feel, express, and ultimately let go of your fear. This can be incredibly empowering and liberating. Once you feel this sense of freedom from your fear—even if it's just a little bit—you can then fill in the mental and emotional space you've created with some positive thoughts, feelings, and desires. How do you do that? Take some time to think about, speak out loud, write down, or even close your eyes and visualize how you want things to be and, more important, how you want to feel. If your fear is focused on something specific like a relationship, visualize it being how you want it to be and allow yourself to feel how you ultimately want to feel. If you're worried about pressure at the office and want to lower your level of stress and anxiety, see and feel yourself being peaceful and calm at what is usually a very tough proposals meeting for example. Whatever it is that you specifically want to happen and however it is you want to feel, focus on that outcome and those emotions. Once you can see it in your mind and feel it in your heart, the chances of you manifesting and experiencing it in reality are greatly increased.

7. Take action. This final stage is an essential one in your fear transformation process. Susan Jeffers is the author of a wonderful best-selling book called *Feel the Fear and Do It Anyway*. What a great mantra for all of us to use and live by. This is true courage! Once you've made your way through all of these stages—confronted, owned, experienced, expressed, and let go of your fear, then visualized how you want things to look and how you want to feel in a positive way—you then have the opportunity to take inspired and courageous action. Your legs may shake, your voice might quiver, but that doesn't have to stop you from saying what's on your mind, taking a risk, making a request, trying something new, or being bold in a small or big way. The more you challenge yourself to take action, even and especially if the action is something that might generate some level of greater fear within you, the more you can build your confidence and send a message to yourself that you can do, say, and be exactly who you are—even if you're initially scared about it. This is how you move though your fear, transform it, and use its energy and power as a catalyst to be authentic.

PRACTICES

The following are a number of powerful practices that you can use in your life to support you in transforming your fear.

1. Breathe. This is a simple but profound practice. Breathing obviously is something we do all day, every day. It's one of many magical aspects of our physical bodies—we can breathe in both an involuntary and a voluntary way. The more you practice conscious breathing and practice taking deep breaths voluntarily on a regular basis, the more you can tap into the power of your breath, your body, and your emotions. Breathing calms us down, lowers our blood pressure, reduces our heart rates, and is a great way to become more aware of our thoughts and feelings in a conscious way. There are books, audios, and classes on breathing and lots of great ways to learn to become more effective in how you breathe. You can look into any of these or you can just take some time to pay more attention to your breath, slow yourself down, and use conscious breathing as a way to move through your fear and be more peaceful in your life.

2. Choose to do new things that scare you. Seek out things that cause fear within you and practice doing them anyway. The more you're able to "feel the fear and do it anyway," the more you'll build your confidence and your capacity for courage. This is not about being crazy or putting undue pressure on yourself, this is about pushing yourself in a way that causes you to grow, stretch, and evolve. You might want to sing karaoke, write something personal or creative and share it with others, build or make something with your hands, give a public talk, go skydiving, or anything else—"big" or "small." Make a list of five or more things that you would be scared to do, but that you know by doing them you'd build up your capacity for courageous action. Once you have your list—start doing them! It's often best to do these things with someone else or at least to have someone to support you and hold you accountable.

3. Give yourself time and space to feel your fear. We're often so busy that we don't give ourselves much down time—especially as it relates to feeling our real feelings. Take some time on a regular basis, maybe when you're already meditating, praying, taking a walk or shower, riding in your car, and so on—and allow yourself to really feel your fear. Again, this is not about worrying in a debilitating way, but rather giving yourself the space and time to experience your fear honestly and emotionally, which is the most essential part in being able to transform it. The more we practice feeling our fear, the more ability we have to move through it with ease.

4. Use the fear transforming technique—write, destroy, visualize. This is a tangible technique that you can use when you're facing some significant fear in your life and you want to transform it and utilize its energy in a positive way. I learned this originally from my counselor Chris Andersonn and use it myself and with others all the time. There are three important steps to this process. Step 1—Write down all of your fears on a piece of paper and do this three separate times. Doing it three times is symbolic; engages your subconscious mind; and allows you to make sure you truly admit, own, feel, and express your fear. Step 2—Destroy all three papers by fire or water—either burn them up or rip them up and flush them down the toilet. As you're destroying these papers, say to yourself, "I'm letting go of and releasing these fears." Step 3—Sit or lay down, close your eyes, relax, and visualize your fears being lifted off of you and transformed into positive energy. When I do this, I often see my fears as wet blankets or garbage being taken off me, burned up, and then transformed into what I want to have happen or how I want to feel. As you complete your visualization, allow yourself to see and feel the specific outcomes and emotions you want to experience in relation to the specific things you're feeling fearful about. In other words, focus on how you want it to go, what you want it to look like, and how you want to feel.

Now that we've looked at the importance of knowing ourselves and transforming our fears—as a pathway to deeper authenticity in our lives, our work, and our relationships—we can move on to Principle 3, Express Yourself, and delve into the power of speaking our truth and expressing our real thoughts and feelings in an authentic way.

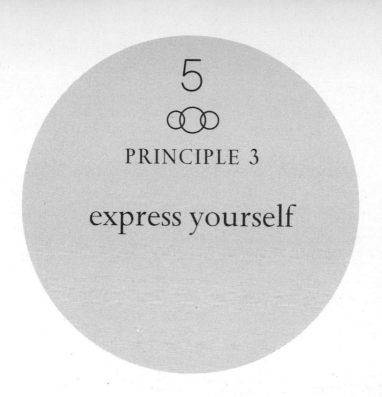

5

PRINCIPLE 3

express yourself

"Be who you are and say what you feel, because those who mind don't matter and those who matter don't mind."

—Dr. Seuss

Fully expressing ourselves is fundamental to our ability to be who we really are and to live with authenticity. However, as we've discussed already, authentic self-expression isn't easy for many of us, given our backgrounds, social conditioning, fears of other people's judgments, and much more. While we all want the people around us to be honest, open, and real, and we in turn want to have the freedom to express ourselves authentically, when the "rubber meets the road" in life, we often hold back our true thoughts and feelings.

With Principle 3, Express Yourself, we'll take a look at how we can fully express ourselves. When we do this—even if it's scary or difficult—we create a sense of freedom, confidence, and realness for ourselves and those around us that is not only liberating but incredibly compelling and rewarding. Expressing ourselves as honestly as we can is one of the most challenging but important things for us to do on our journey of growth and discovery, as we embody greater authenticity in our lives.

Speaking Our Truth

How honest are you? While most of us aren't bald-faced liars who go around deceiving people consciously, if we're honest with ourselves about it, we often don't fully speak our truth. It can be scary and vulnerable, we aren't usually trained or encouraged to do so, and it often seems "inappropriate" to be totally transparent in many situations and relationships. A great metaphor for this phenomenon is that of an iceberg—usually only the "tip of the iceberg" is visible on the surface of the water, while the majority of it exists underneath the waterline.

This is often how we go through life—just showing the tip of our own personal icebergs. This dynamic is understandable, normal, and encouraged in our culture, but it doesn't allow us to express fully who we are in a real way. What it takes for us to live our lives, have relationships, and do our work at a deeper level of authenticity is for us to lower that waterline, share more of who we really are, and speak our truth courageously.

Getting Real

Being able and willing to lower our personal "waterlines" is something we can do to be real in all aspects of our lives. What's down below your waterline that you often don't want to share with others or speak about out loud?

Here are some of the things that are often below our waterlines:

- Failures
- Opinions (we worry aren't shared by others)
- Confusion
- Shame
- Guilt
- Fears
- Anger
- Insecurities
- Weakness
- Embarrassment
- Judgments (of others and ourselves)
- Challenges
- Resentment
- Jealousy
- Loneliness

- And lots of other stuff we don't think is "acceptable" for people to know about us or for us to express

Most of these are things we consider to be "bad." However, if we think about it more deeply, there are also lots of things below our waterlines that are more positive, even if they're still sometimes challenging for us to share with others, such as the following:

- Hopes
- Dreams
- Passions
- Visions
- Happiness
- Accomplishments
- Goals
- Love
- Appreciation
- Excitement
- Gratitude
- Curiosity
- Creativity
- And other "positive" stuff we're often hesitant to share because of what we fear the perception or judgment of us might be

Whether we think something about us or our lives is "bad" or "good," there are lots of things we consider to be "out of bounds" for us to share with others. I'm not advocating that we must tell everyone everything about ourselves, but I do believe that for us to be who we really are and to live with a deeper sense of authenticity, it's essential that we start to share more of ourselves. This can be scary and challenging, but it's one of the best ways for us to get real and to tap into the power and freedom of authenticity.

However, it's important to remember that getting real and sharing our true feelings are not about us complaining, "trauma sharing" (a manipulative way to get attention from others or play the role of "victim" in life), feeling sorry for ourselves, or even bragging—all of which, while common, are usually ego-based and unhealthy. The key elements of authentic sharing are honesty, responsibility, and, most important, vulnerability. When we're real, take responsibility for how we feel (not blame it on others or uncontrollable circumstances), and share ourselves in a vulnerable way—we can tap into the true power of authenticity.

Being Honest and Vulnerable

Two of the most authentic and inspiring people I know are Rich and Yvonne St. John-Dutra. They're my dear friends, teachers, and the cofounders of an incredible organization called Challenge Day, which delivers life-altering, experiential, personal development workshops for teens, schools, and people of all ages. As friends, as mentors, and through their workshops, Rich and Yvonne have taught me so much about life, relationships, growth, and especially authenticity.

They introduced me to the iceberg metaphor and use it as a key element in all of their work. One of the most powerful exercises from their Challenge Day workshops is called "If You Really Knew Me." This exercise, which has had a profound impact on my own life and is something I've facilitated in various forms with many of the groups and individuals I've coached over the years, gives people an incredible opportunity to get real and vulnerable. How it works is that each person in the group—usually a smallish group of anywhere from four to eight people (although it can be done one-on-one or with a larger group)—gets a minute or two of undivided attention from everyone else in the group and repeats this sentence, "If you really knew me, you'd know . . ." and then completes the sentence by sharing things that are real, vulnerable, and below the waterline about themselves (thoughts, feelings, dreams, insecurities, opinions, passions, and so on).

There's no pressure or expectation on each person to share anything they don't want to share—just a challenge to step outside of their comfort zones; choose to trust the people in the group; and be more open, real, and vulnerable than they may normally be with others. For this exercise to work, it's essential that people feel safe and know that what they say will be held in confidence, and that the other people in the group do everything they can to pay full attention and honor each person as they share their true thoughts and feelings.

Whenever I either participate in or facilitate this exercise, I'm always amazed by its power. People laugh, cry, get real, let go of things they've been holding onto, and truly connect with each other—heart to heart and in an authentic way. And while some individuals and groups are willing to go deeper than others, and in some cases this activity is more of a stretch or challenge than in others, I've never seen it not work. Remarkable things happen—people are able to understand, get to know, and have real compassion for one another—even if they've just met or don't think they have anything in common. What I always get from this exercise myself and hear people say in different ways is that even though we're all unique, we're way more alike than we are different. When we have the courage to get real with each other and speak our truth, it's one of the most meaningful, rewarding, and connecting experiences we can have with other human beings.

If You Really Knew Me . . .

As a way of modeling this exercise, getting more real, and being vulnerable, and so that you can know more about who I am, I will lower my own waterline right here, as if we were sitting together in a group and doing this powerful exercise.

If you really knew me, you'd know that as excited and honored as I am to be writing this book, talking about authenticity, and working with people to be more real and fulfilled in their lives, it's incredibly challenging and scary for me to do this. I doubt myself all the time, and sometimes think I don't really know what heck I'm talking about. Even worse, I'm constantly worried that people will see right through me, that they will find out that I actually struggle big time to practice what I teach, and that many aspects of my life, my work, and my relationships aren't filled with authenticity, appreciation, or fulfillment as much as I'd like them to be.

If you really, really knew me, you'd know that sometimes I hate myself—so much so that at times it's even hard for me to look at myself in the mirror or focus on anything except for all the things I think are wrong with me. I judge myself, my body and appearance, what I say, how I act, and the ways I interact with people in an incredibly mean and harsh way. I can be hypercritical of almost every aspect of myself. I often feel like a total loser and a complete fraud. Even though I "know" better, there's a part of me that thinks in order for me to be okay and to be loved I have to be super successful in my career, look great physically, have it all together, and be someone that people universally admire and respect.

And if you really, really, really knew me, you'd know that I have a big vision for my life and my work that is incredibly sacred to me. I believe I'm on my spiritual path and am here to do important work. I know I have the ability to heal myself and grow, to help others heal themselves and grow, and to support in the healing and growth of our world. I'm often uncomfortable to admit this because I worry that it sounds arrogant, grandiose, or self-important; that people will judge me; that it may cause me to uproot my life or my family, to work harder than I really want to work, or to do things that are more challenging or scary than I think I'm capable of; or that my ego will take over (as it often does), run with it, and make it all about money, book sales, fame, and notoriety. Because of my own fear and confusion about this, I often sell out, don't fully go for what I want, and don't speak my truth at the deepest level—even though it might look like I do on the surface.

 EXERCISE
If You Really Knew Me . . .

Now it's your turn to lower your waterline! There are a few different ways you can do this exercise, and while it's okay to start with thinking, writing, or speaking just to and for yourself, ultimately it's about sharing your truth with others—as many as you can and in a way that will best serve your growth and desire to be real. Here are a few options of how you can do this exercise.

Option 1

Take out your journal; find a piece of paper; or open up a file, e-mail, or blog page on your computer. At the top of the page write, "If you really knew me . . ." and then start writing anything and everything you have the courage to share—anger, passions, fears, dreams, guilt, accomplishments, failures, goals, or anything else that is real and vulnerable. Once you're done writing, share it with others—by e-mail, on the Web, by having people read it to themselves, or by you reading it to them.

Option 2

Sit down with your spouse, significant other, family member, friend, boss, co-worker, or anyone else—ideally in person, but on the phone if you don't live close to them—and have an honest conversation with them one-on-one. It may be a good idea to let them know something about this book, the iceberg metaphor, or your commitment to being real and authentic first so that they know where you're coming from and what your intention is. Once you set it up, start with, "If you really knew me . . ." and then share with them as much as you can from a deep, vulnerable, and honest place within you. It's often a good idea to give yourself a time limit (just a few minutes) and also to ask them to not interrupt you, ask questions, or interject—which usually makes it safer and easier all the way around. They may want to respond to what you say specifically, and they also may be interested in doing their own session of "If you really knew me . . ."

Option 3

Do this activity with a group of friends, your family, your work team, or any group of people. It usually works best with a group of between four and eight, but can be done with any number. It's essential to let everyone know what you're doing, why you're doing it, and how it will go. Using the iceberg analogy and even drawing a picture of it on a flip chart or whiteboard is often a good idea with a group as well. For this exercise to work in a group, it's vital that people feel safe and supported, and that they can trust that what they say will be held sacred and in confidence. It's also always best if you go first—people will follow your lead, so the more you're willing to lower your waterline, the more likely others will do so in a real and authentic way.

Letting Go and Moving Forward

Another question I asked lots of people—friends, family members, clients, and others—as I was preparing to write this book was, "What's an example of a time in your life when you said something important from a deep place of truth within you and it had an incredibly positive impact (in other words, you were true to yourself—even if you were scared or it was hard—and it really worked out)?" Once again, the responses to this question were fascinating. While every answer was unique, the primary themes of most people's responses had to do with being able to let go of something from the past and to move forward to a new type of relationship with a specific person or a whole new type of life in general. Following are two of the responses I got. Jennifer said,

> Growing up, my mother was not nurturing at all. I could literally be standing in front of her crying, and she wouldn't comfort me. My takeaway for many years was that crying was a sign of weakness and that weakness was bad. To seek my mother's approval, I felt I had to be very strong and never cry. This was an insanely difficult task for me, as I was always very passionate and emotional as a youth and it felt very "inauthentic" to me to be anything but. However, I constantly strove to be stronger.

After I went through some therapy and realized that there wasn't anything wrong with me for crying, I finally confronted my mother about it when I was in my late twenties. It took all of my strength and courage to do so. During a long car trip, just the two of us, I asked her why she never comforted me when I cried. She shared with me that since her own mother was very fragile and always crying that she was afraid that I would turn out like her. She said she was trying to make me strong. It was eye opening for me because I realized that my mother's actions had nothing to do with me. It was also the first time I was able to speak up and really be authentic with her, as opposed to always trying to please her. It was a powerful moment in my life and in our relationship.

Terces said,

I'd been asked by my family physician to keep his abusing me a secret and of course I did. He had a wife and family, and was a Naval officer. I'd been taught to obey my elders and certainly to do what they said. I was sixteen years old at the time. I did keep it a secret and developed a severe eating disorder that I suffered with for twenty years. One day I heard my internal wisdom tell me to tell the truth. I couldn't imagine doing that after all those years. I was currently married to a Naval officer myself and was afraid of what my truth would mean to my marriage, my children, and my parents. I wondered if anyone would believe me.

I did tell the truth and people did get angry, disappointed, and some didn't believe me. However, I felt free for the first time I could remember. I actually changed my name to Terces, which spells "secret" backwards, as a symbol of the importance not to keep secrets, but to be honest and forthcoming with the truth. I wasn't the kind of person who would change their name so it was actually a big challenge for me to do that.

My life did change dramatically after that and all for the better, although it may not have looked like it to others. I started to heal myself, believe in myself, trust myself, and love myself. It has now been over twenty years since I told the truth, and every day someone asks me about my name. I don't always tell them the whole story, but it is a constant reminder of the importance of being truthful to myself.

Resolving Conflict

The more we embrace being real and speaking our truth, the more effectively we're able to engage in and resolve conflict in a healthy, honest, and productive way. However, when you hear the word conflict, what immediately comes to mind? For me and most people I know, the thoughts, words, feelings, and ideas that initially come up related to conflict are things such as

- Fight
- Disagreement
- War
- Anger

- Frustration
- Power struggle
- Uncomfortable
- Confrontation
- Yelling

However, if we go a little deeper and look at the positive benefits of having conflict, especially when it gets resolved, what kinds of things come to mind for you about that? For me and from what others say in my workshops, it's often things such as

- Resolution
- New ideas
- Understanding
- Trust
- Bonding
- Creativity
- Awareness
- Teamwork
- Confidence
- Relief

The reality is that conflict has lots of positive aspects to it, especially if we're able to engage in it in a straightforward manner. Most of the things we think of in a negative sense about conflict come down to one big thing—fear! Ah yes, fear again. The majority of people I work with and talk to, including me, get scared when it comes to conflict and have lots of creative, elaborate, and often passive-aggressive tactics to avoid dealing with conflict, like being "nice," pretending everything is "fine," talking to others about the issue instead of dealing with it directly, not speaking up, "biting their tongue," and more. Even those who have a tendency to pick a fight, like to argue and debate, and seem to have no problem "getting into it" with others usually do this as their strategy for dealing with conflict, and more specifically their fear of conflict.

Danger and Opportunity

The Chinese symbol for conflict is a great reminder to all of us about the true nature of conflict. The first character in the symbol represents "danger" while the second one represents "opportunity."

Isn't this true? We fear the danger, but hope for the opportunity. This is actually a great metaphor for life, dealing with fear, and being authentic in general. The only way to get to the good stuff, in this case the "opportunity" or resolution of the conflict, is to face the "danger" of our fear of what might be done, said, or thought about us in the process of addressing the issue.

The question is not whether we'll have conflict in our lives, our work, and our relationships—the question is how willing and able we are to deal with our conflicts in an authentic and effective way.

CHECK THIS OUT
The Importance of Conflict

According to author, consultant, and leadership expert Patrick Lencioni, author of the best-selling book *The Five Dysfunctions of a Team,* "All great relationships, the ones that last over time, require productive conflict in order to grow. This is true in marriage, parenthood, friendship, and business."

Steps We Can Take to Resolve Conflicts
Authentically and Effectively

Whenever we're facing a conflict with a spouse, significant other, child, family member, friend, co-worker, boss, vendor, client, service person, stranger, or even a group or team we belong to or work with, there are only two ways to resolve the conflict effectively and authentically.

First, we can deal with conflict directly and honestly until it's completely resolved. This sometimes can take a while, be uncomfortable, or even get ugly before it gets worked out. But as we all know and have experienced, it's not only possible but incredibly empowering when we do work though our conflicts with others directly and honestly.

The second way we can work out a conflict is to completely let it go. This doesn't mean that we pretend to forget about it or that we talk about it to others while acting "nice" to the person with whom we have the conflict. This means we totally let it go and release its power and impact on us, on our relationship with that person, and on our lives. Once again, we all have lots of experience with this as we've let go of way more conflicts in our lives than we've hung onto—even though it's the ones we hang onto that get most of our attention.

Sadly, in most cases we end up choosing "door number three," which isn't one of the two ways we can effectively resolve a conflict. We may try to address it directly, but when it doesn't go well, we get scared, or it doesn't look like we can get our way—we pull back and start talking to others about it in order to prove how "right" we are and how "wrong" the other person is. Or we may attempt to let it go, but as soon as something remotely close to the same issue pops up again, we're right back into the conflict and use it as more evidence against the other person or situation we were upset about to begin with.

Assuming we want to address and resolve our conflicts authentically, even though this can be challenging and scary for us to do, there are some specific steps we can take and things we can remember that will allow us to engage in the conflict in the most effective and authentic way possible.

1. Take responsibility. It always "takes two to tango." Taking responsibility is not about being at fault or blaming the other person, it's about owning up to the situation and recognizing that we are a part of the issue—even though in most cases we think we're "right" and they're "wrong."

If we remember that we aren't victims, that we're responsible for our reactions and emotions, and that true resolution of a conflict isn't about one person winning and the other person losing, we can enter into the conflict from a responsible and authentic perspective that will allow us to be open enough to resolve it effectively.

2. Address the conflict or issue directly. Conflicts are always handled most successfully when they're dealt with directly and promptly. It's also important to honor people's time, space, mood, personality, and priorities when addressing a conflict with them. The best approach is to let them know in an honest way that we have something important to talk to them about and ask their permission to have the conversation. Being real, vulnerable, and "lowering our waterline" as we engage in a conflict is also essential. If I'm feeling scared, uncomfortable, or at all awkward about engaging in a conflict or difficult conversation with someone, which I usually am, I'll often acknowledge those feelings as honestly as possible at the start, which then sets an authentic tone for our conversation.

3. Seek first to understand. Regardless of the situation, circumstance, or how the conflict unfolds or comes up, we often get defensive and want to tell our side of the story. While this is a totally normal phenomenon, it's always best for us to stop and listen to the other person and do what we can to understand where he or she is coming from. Each person involved in every conflict usually has a very clear, rational, and understandable reason they did what they did, said what they said, or feel how they feel—at least from their perspective. Without having to agree or disagree with them, when we do whatever we can to see things from their perspective, chances are we'll not only understand them better and connect with them more effectively, we'll more likely be able to resolve the conflict in a productive and authentic way.

4. Use "I" statements. Saying to someone, "You shouldn't have said that, it was rude" may be our honest opinion. However, that statement is a judgment and an accusation—which is usually true for almost any statement beginning with the word "you." By using "I" statements, being specific, and being real, our words and feedback have more power and can lead to resolution. Changing the statement above to, "When you said that, I got upset and it hurt my feelings," changes the dynamic, feeling, and impact of what's being said. "I" statements are always true (assuming we're being authentic), and they can't really be argued with or debated. If someone does or says something and I have a specific reaction to it, that's real. If I judge someone, make a generalization about them, or accuse them of something, not only is it not "true" (it's just my opinion) it will most likely trigger a defensive response from them.

5. Go for a win-win. The only real way to have a conflict resolved authentically is if it's a true win-win for everyone involved. This doesn't mean that each person gets his or her way, which in many cases can't happen simply because of the nature of our conflicts and the circumstances of life and relationships. It does, however, mean that everyone gets heard, honored, and listened to. And it's essential that we alter our perspective and paradigm for conflicts from one of winning and losing to one of understanding and collaboration. When we relate to our conflicts from the perspective of traditional "winning," we either come out ahead or behind, but someone always loses—which can damage relationships and create deep divides between people. When we can make sure that everyone involved has a sense of completion—meaning they have nothing more to say and have a sense of acceptance for the outcome—even if they don't agree with it completely—then a win-win becomes possible and the conflict can not only get resolved but bring people closer together in the process.

6. Acknowledge them. Whether it's a one-on-one conversation or a situation that involves lots of people, acknowledgment is essential to our ability to engage in productive conflict and to be able to resolve it in an authentic and effective way. If someone is willing to share their honest feelings with us, give us some vulnerable feedback, or be open to having a difficult conversation with us—those are all things we can acknowledge them for. When someone gives me critical feedback or even when they're angry with me, as much as I don't usually like it in the moment, I always try to genuinely thank them for being real because I know it's not easy to do that and that they're probably feeling a little scared or uncomfortable about it. Even if it's hard to hear or swallow, I try to take critical feedback as a sign of respect and a way of honoring me and my relation-ship to them. When we can acknowledge the other peo-ple we're in conflict with, we remind them that we're all in this together and that who they are matters as much or more than the "issue" we're in conflict about.

Following these steps will make it easier for us to resolve conflict in a successful and authentic way. And when we remember that almost everyone we're in conflict with, like us, is a bit scared and uncomfortable about being in the conflict, we can put our attention on having com-passion (for them and for ourselves), being vulnerable, and relating to the conflict in the most authentic and respon-sible way possible.

Conflict Resolution in Action

I was hired to facilitate a meeting for the senior execu-tive group for one of my corporate clients. The organization had grown rapidly and was doing well, but there were some issues, conflicts, and personality challenges within their senior team—specifically related to the president and CEO, Paul.

Paul was super smart, and people on his team and within the entire company, which consisted of about 1,700 people, seemed to like him. However, the feedback I got from most of the people on his team prior to the meet-ing was that he didn't do a great job listening to them or communicating the vision of where he wanted things to go, and that overall many of them felt his leadership skills were lacking. A number of people on the team also felt pretty intimidated by Paul and said he wasn't all that good at receiving feedback.

The meeting started and we had a packed agenda—going over goals, talking about some organizational issues, and making plans for the upcoming fiscal year. About an hour into it, things weren't going very well—not only were we off track with the agenda, but the discussion was getting heated, people were cutting each other off, and the overall feeling in the room wasn't very open or positive.

Even though I wasn't planning to do this and was a little hesitant at first, I stopped the discussion, introduced the iceberg metaphor, and set up the "If you really knew me . . ." exercise. Although the group had twelve people in it, I thought it would be best for us to do the exercise all together. I went first and shared as authentically as I could about feeling intimidated by them (since they were such a senior team, so smart, and so successful), frustrated about how things were going so far, and also hopeful that we could all get more real and have a productive meeting.

As each person took their turn after me and started to lower their "waterline," I could feel things start to change in the room—it was visceral. People got real and opened up about personal stuff in their lives, how they were feeling in the moment, and what they wanted—both with the meeting and in general. Two of the people in the group actually cried, which although a bit awkward and uncomfortable for them and some others in the group at first, really opened things up that much more. When we got done with the exercise—less than twenty minutes later—it felt like a totally different group.

Then Jerry, one of the members of the team who'd expressed real frustration about Paul to me when we talked and also had emphasized how intimidated he was by him, raised his hand.

"Can I share something?" he asked.

"Sure, Jerry, go right ahead," I replied.

"I'm a little scared to say this, but I think it's important. I've been feeling frustrated for quite a while, as some of you know, about a number of things related to our team and company. I realized just now that I don't usually speak up at meetings because I'm worried about saying the wrong thing or getting in trouble. Paul—I love working for this company and being on this team, but I want to know more about where we're headed. I feel like I'm in the dark half the time and I want more communication from you. I don't really know how to say this to you without feeling like I'm stepping out of line or worrying about you yelling at me, which has happened a few times in the past and left me feeling upset and embarrassed. I'm sorry for not bringing this up sooner and hope it's not inappropriate for me to say in front of everyone here at this meeting—but I just felt I had to speak about this honestly."

A hush fell over the room. People's eyes got big, and I could tell that everyone, including Paul and Jerry, were stunned at what had just been said. After a long pregnant pause, Paul responded.

He said, "Wow Jerry, I had no idea you felt that way. Do other people feel like Jerry?" asked Paul.

Most of the heads in the room nodded and a few people even raised their hands.

"Really?" Paul exclaimed, both stunned and a little annoyed. "I wish you all would have said something earlier," he said.

Susie, another member of the team, said, "We've tried a few times, but it hasn't felt like you were all that interested in our feedback. And, like Jerry mentioned, those of us who've said things in the past have often felt intimidated or reprimanded for doing so."

Paul then looked at everyone around the table and said, "I'm sorry! I have a tendency to get really focused on the numbers and forget about people. Even with all of our success in recent years, I constantly worry about us failing, falling short, or regressing—so I keep pushing. I guess I don't do such a great job of letting you all know where we're headed or allowing you to let me know how you feel, what you want, and if there's anything I'm doing that isn't working. I can be a little stubborn sometimes."

With that honest admission, everyone, including Paul, burst out laughing. Over the next few hours, a number of important issues were discussed, ideas were shared, goals were set, and decisions were made. According to a number of people in the group, it was one of the most productive meetings they'd ever had. Over the next few months, as I continued to consult with this team and company, their communication improved and they came together in a successful way. It wasn't that things magically changed and their conflicts vanished, it was that they created an environment of authenticity and open communication that allowed them to speak more freely, be more real, and deal with things directly.

Expressing All of Our Emotions

Being able to acknowledge, make peace with, and express our emotions—all of them—is an essential aspect of being who we are and being authentic in life. However, this is another thing we've not been trained to do. As we discussed in Chapter One, our culture and most of the people around us don't encourage the passionate expression of many of our emotions, especially the ones that are considered "bad," such as anger, fear, sadness, hurt, shame, guilt, grief, sorrow, and others. Excitement, joy, love, happiness, and gratitude are okay, but they're often met with cynicism, and even these "good" ones are only encouraged to be expressed in "appropriate" ways and for "appropriate" reasons.

A Different Way to Relate to Our Emotions

The more able we are to fully express our emotions, the more freedom and power we have, and the more real we can be. From a deeper perspective, it's helpful for us to think of emotions being "positive" when they're effectively expressed and released and "negative" when they're denied, avoided, or repressed.

We've all had experiences when we expressed an emotion that we usually consider to be "negative," such as fear, anger, or sadness, and in our expression of it something wonderful happened—we felt a sense of relief, we let go of something we were holding onto, we worked out an issue or conflict in a relationship, and so on. This is why we often feel so wonderful and liberated after a good, deep cry.

We've also all had experiences with emotions that we consider to be "positive," such as love or gratitude, and our inability to express them. As a result, we may have suppressed these emotions, which ultimately had a negative impact on us and others. In addition, the denial and avoidance of many of our most intense emotions such as rage, guilt, anger, shame, fear, and others have been scientifically linked to many of the most painful degenerative diseases facing human beings today, including cancer, arthritis, heart disease, and many more.

If we remember that being aware of our emotions, owning them, experiencing them, and finding healthy ways to express them is the real goal—not just having emotions we think are "good" or avoiding the ones we think are "bad"—we can create a new and empowered relationship to our emotions and to our true selves. Making peace with our emotions and being able and willing to express them all is a key element to living an authentic life.

Healthy Ways to Express Our Emotions

Finding healthy, real, and safe ways for us to express our emotions is important as we become more authentic in our lives. The most important things for us to remember about expressing our emotions are, first of all, that we can always move through them if we're willing to admit them, own them, feel them, and fully express them. And, second of all, the more we allow ourselves to just experience and express our emotions, without judging them, the more authentic, healthy, and fulfilled we'll be in life.

Both speaking and writing in an authentic way can be healthy and empowering ways for us to honestly express our emotions. When we talk about our feelings to others or write them down it's important that we check in with ourselves to make sure we're actually feeling and expressing our real emotions, as a way to move through them, not just talking or writing about them conceptually. Here are a two other healthy and productive ways we can authentically express our emotions.

- **Scream, yell, jump around, let it out.** Most of us have done this at points in our lives and definitely when we were children. Allowing ourselves to emote in a passionate way—whether we're excited, sad, in love, scared, joyful, angry, or anything else—is a great way to express ourselves. We don't do this so much as adults because we worry about what other people will think of us and don't think it's "appropriate." The key is to pay attention to how we're feeling and allow those feelings to come out. If you feel like laughing, laugh. If you feel like crying, cry. Doing this with a group of people, facilitated in a workshop with trained leaders who have experience, or being somewhere away from others who might get scared or have a reaction to our emotional expression can be very helpful. Being able to express ourselves fully and in our own unique way is the ultimate goal. I sometimes like to scream at the top of my lungs when I'm feeling excited or when I'm feeling angry, and I will often do this in my car so as to not freak other people out. When I'm feeling sad, because I've trained myself for most of my life to suppress my feelings (like many of us, especially men), I will sometimes purposely do things, talk to people, and think about things that will bring out some emotion in me, allowing me to cry and release that sadness. Beating on pillows, jumping up and down, or shaking our bodies around in an authentic expression of emotion can also be powerful to get us to release whatever emotions we are feeling. However, we must be safe when we do this, hence doing it with the support and guidance of others is helpful. Authentic emotional expression takes practice, support, and awareness—but is a great way to get real and move through your emotions.

- **Meditate, pray, go within.** Since all of our emotions and most of the conflicts we deal with in our lives are actually internal, one of the best and most powerful ways for us to express our emotions is to do it through meditation, with prayer, or by simply going within ourselves. This is a very personal process and will vary based on our belief systems and personalities. This is not about suppressing our emotions—quite the opposite—but it is about expressing and releasing them through our connection with something within ourselves or greater than ourselves—some call this our Higher Self, Inner Guidance, Soul, Spirit, or nothing at all. What you call it and how to relate to it isn't as important as being able to express and release your emotions personally. I will often lie down, close my eyes, and visualize a person I'm angry with, scared of, or upset with, and in my mind I'll have a conversation with them—expressing all of my honest thoughts and feelings. As powerful as it can be to have that conversation with that person in the "real" world, I've found it to be equally and sometimes more powerful to have it with them metaphysically (in my mind), because my ego and my fear of their reaction don't get in the way. The goal is to acknowledge, feel, and express the emotion authentically so we can learn from it and move through it. Doing this in meditation, prayer, or within our own minds and hearts can be incredibly effective—if we do it in a genuine and authentic way.

PRACTICES

The following are a number of powerful practices that you can use in your life to support you in expressing yourself in an authentic and liberating way. A number of these practices are designed for you to do with others and will encourage a deeper level of authenticity and connection with the people in your life.

1. "Check in" first. When you start a meeting, a date, a meal, or an important conversation, take a moment and have everyone involved in that meeting or conversation "check in." This means that you lower your waterline and share a little about how you're feeling and what's going on with you in an authentic way. You may want to do the "If you really knew me . . ." exercise completely or you may just want to give yourself and others a moment each to share some real thoughts and feelings. I try to always do this with groups I work with, meetings I facilitate, and even sometimes when I'm with Michelle or getting together with friends.

2. Make a list of your conflicts: deal with them or let them go. Write down all of the issues, conflicts, withheld communications, resentments, and more that you currently have. After you complete your list, look back over it and first ask yourself, "Which of these am I willing to let go of?" Be honest with yourself, and if you can authentically let any of them go, do so—it will free you up and make you feel so much better. Letting go is not about denial or avoidance, it's about freedom and taking responsibility. For example, you might realize that an issue you have with a friend, family member, or co-worker that you've been holding onto really isn't that big of a deal after all and that you can just let it go. Remember this wonderful saying, "Holding a grudge is like drinking poison and expecting the other person to die." For the ones you aren't willing or able to let go of, ask yourself this question: "What can I do or say to resolve this conflict?" You may not know. You may have tried. You may not be willing to actually do what it will take. Whatever the case may be, I challenge you to step outside of your comfort zone and do or say whatever you think will have each conflict on your list get resolved. Use the steps laid out earlier in this chapter.

3. Release your "withholds." A "withhold" is something you've been holding onto with another person that you haven't shared with them—hurt, resentment, fear, an apology, an acknowledgment, or anything else. Creating the time and space to communicate these "withholds" is an incredibly powerful and liberating thing to do, even though it can be a little scary. Michelle and I do this on a regular basis. You can do it with your spouse, friends, family, co-workers, or anyone else. One person goes first and says to the other person (or to one specific person if you're doing this in a group), "There's something I've withheld from you." The other person responds by saying, "Okay, would you like to tell me?" Then the first person expresses his or her "withhold" with as much honesty, vulnerability, and responsibility as possible (using "I" statements, owning their feelings, and so on). The other person's job is to listen with as much openness as possible, not to react, and to just say "thank you" when the person is done. It's best to do this back and forth until both people (or everyone in the group) has shared all of their withholds. When you're done, one or both of you may want to talk about some of the things that were said, but that isn't always necessary. This is not about debate or someone being right or wrong, this is about being able to share how you're feeling and what you've been withholding as a way to release it. At some level, each "withhold," regardless of what it is, isn't really about the other person anyway, it's about you (or vice versa).

4. Find someone to support you in expressing your emotions. We all can benefit from support, guidance, and feedback—in general and specifically with expressing our emotions. It doesn't really matter if it's a friend, counselor, support group, coach, co-worker, family member, or your spouse or significant other—what matters is that you can be real with this person; can fully express your emotions with them; and can allow and empower them to push you, give you feedback, and support you emotionally. Remember, this is not about you "complaining" or "venting," per se, it's more about you authentically expressing your emotions in a way that has you take responsibility for them and move through them. Also, there are so many wonderful people out there in your life and in the world who are great at supporting the authentic expression of emotions—go find someone (or many people) who specifically can help you express your emotions in a real and liberating way.

Now that we've looked at the importance of knowing ourselves, transforming our fears, and fully expressing ourselves, we're ready to move to our next principle, Be Bold, and look at how we can boldly live, speak, and act in ways that are true to our deepest passions and our most authentic selves.

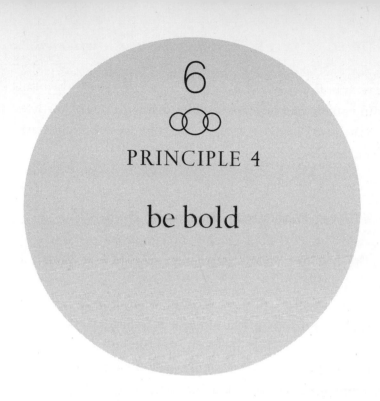

6

PRINCIPLE 4

be bold

"Don't ask what the world needs. Ask what makes you come alive, and go do it. Because what the world needs is people who have come alive."

—Howard Thurman

Being bold is one of the most essential aspects of authenticity. We're not often trained or encouraged to be bold in life. Living our lives in a bold and authentic way takes real courage and commitment. This doesn't mean that we won't get scared, it simply means that we're willing to act in the face of our fear and able to stay true to ourselves and what's important to us, even when it gets difficult.

In this chapter we'll take a look at what it truly means to be bold and how we can live this way in our daily lives. When we have the courage to be bold, we're both liberated and inspired by the power of authenticity.

What Does It Mean to Be Bold?

The first two definitions of the word bold on Dictionary .com are

- Not hesitating or fearful in the face of actual or possible danger or rebuff; courageous and daring: *a bold hero*.
- Not hesitating to break the rules of propriety; forward; impudent: *He apologized for being so bold as to speak to the emperor.*

While these definitions make sense and do describe the general concept of boldness, the practice of being bold in each of our lives is unique. What might be bold for me based on my personality, background, belief system, strengths, fears, and more may not be bold for you. And, like authenticity itself, what it means for each of us to be bold changes as we grow and evolve.

In the context of our discussion about authenticity, being bold is about stepping up and stepping out onto our "edge" in life—pushing the limits of what we think is possible or appropriate. It's about living, speaking, and acting in ways that are both courageous and true to who we really are. It's not necessarily about being provocative or controversial just for the sake of it, although it may involve those things. For example, I could dye my hair green, take off all of my clothes, and run around the streets where I live. However, since doing this doesn't really express anything authentic about who I am or what's important to me, it's not really a bold act—weird, scary, and even fun maybe, but not bold.

Being bold, as it relates to being ourselves and living with authenticity, has to do with us getting in touch with our deepest truths, passions, and desires in life and then having the courage to live and act "out loud" in a way that is congruent with this.

How to Be Bold

Being bold takes a great deal of practice and courage. Boldness can be difficult because by its nature there will always be a sense of fear and challenge involved in any bold action we take or bold approach to life. With this in mind, there are several things we can do and practice to increase our willingness and ability to be bold—in our relationships, our work, and our lives.

The following pages address five of the most important aspects of being bold in life:

1. Be true to yourself
2. Live with passion
3. Step out

4. Lean on others
5. When you fall down, get back up

By remembering and practicing all five of these, you'll be able to live your life with a deeper sense of boldness and ultimately authenticity.

Be True to Yourself

Steve Jobs, chairman and CEO of Apple Computer, said in his 2005 commencement address at Stanford University, "Don't let the noise of other people's opinions drown out your own inner voice."

In Part One of this book, we discussed the many forces outside and within us that keep us from being ourselves. Specifically, we often think about, listen to, and worry about the opinions and judgments of others so much that we forget about the most important person for us to please and impress—ourselves! It's normal and understandable that we're attached to the opinions of others—we all are and always will be to some degree. I wish I could say I had no attachment whatsoever to your opinion of this book, but that wouldn't be true. The truth is, however, the less attached we are to other people's opinions, the more likely we are to be true to ourselves, which is what allows us to live with real authenticity.

Being true to ourselves takes courage, introspection, and a commitment to tell the truth—to ourselves and to others. We must also remain in a constant inquiry with ourselves about who we are and what's most important to us. This doesn't mean that we never fall short, make mistakes, do or say things that are out of alignment with who we are, change our minds, or get sidetracked in various ways. Of course these things will happen. They're all part of being human. However, when we live our lives true to who we really are, it's okay for us to admit when we've made a mistake, gone off course, or done something that's out of integrity with ourselves. This process is about being honest and forgiving with ourselves and with others in ways that are both fierce and compassionate.

A great example of people being true to themselves and expressing real boldness was how my friend David and his ex-wife ended their marriage. Here's what David had to say about it:

> In 2002, the divorce of my ex-wife and I was about to be finalized. Somehow, during the course of our fourteen years together, we'd moved from our truly magical, mystical, passionate and ground-breaking connection filled with laughter and adventure into a disassociated, alienated, painful experience of silent suffering, door-slamming, and finally infidelity. Although my heart was shattered and I was not functional for a time, either socially or professionally, we chose to listen to our inner guidance and found access to our wedding vows, to always remain friends from the deepest place in our hearts.
>
> So my ex-wife and I decided to have a "Marriage Completion Ceremony," (somewhat like a wedding, but more like a funeral for our marriage).

We met several times, and in the logistics planning, creating of invitations, ceremony writing, etc. both of us actually began to experience the healing that we intended. We did this before fifty of our closest friends and family. The ceremony was filled with tears, music, laughter, and prayers—the poetry of life.

By the end of the ceremony, we had truly "completed" that part of our lives, and my soul has been freer ever since.

I attended this remarkable ceremony, and it was like nothing I'd ever been to before. Yes, it was quite unconventional, but there was something very powerful about both David and his ex-wife being themselves and being public with their pain, their process, and their divorce. They celebrated their relationship, acknowledged their breakup, honored and appreciated each other, and expressed the myriad emotions they were both feeling authentically.

Talk about bold. Creating a sacred ceremony for a divorce is something most people would consider taboo or downright strange.

Because they did this as an expression of who they are and in a unique and heartfelt way, it was not only a bold act of authenticity, it also had a profound impact on those of us who were there. It gave me and many of the people I talked to after the ceremony an opportunity to look at, think about, and face something universal and often quite painful (the end of a love relationship). I was proud of them for doing it, honored to be included, and grateful for the example of boldness.

Live with Passion

Passion is an important part of being bold and living with authenticity. However, we often have some misconceptions about passion and where it comes from.

What are you most passionate about? Where does your passion for these things come from? On the surface, it often looks like the passion in our lives comes from the activities, people, or things we're passionate about. However, this isn't really the case. While it's true that certain people, situations, and activities can make it easier for us to access passion within us—all of the passion we've ever experienced in our lives has come from one place and one place only—us!

Fundamentally, passion is a "below the line" phenomenon. Therefore we each have the ability to generate authentic passion at any time and for any reason. Why is this important? Passion is a key element in our ability to be bold in life. Living an authentic life is about going for it, not holding back, and giving ourselves fully to our work, our relationships, and our lives. We don't have to wait until things line up perfectly, until we have the right circumstances or situation, or until we have everything in our lives mapped out in order to be passionate. Passion is a powerful emotion, but it's also a state of being that we can choose at any time in our lives.

For example, I worked with a woman a few years ago named Susan. She wanted some career coaching and decided to hire me. Susan was in her early fifties and had spent more than fifteen years at home raising her three kids. She'd been back in the professional world for just a few years and was working as marketing assistant for a big consulting firm. Although she'd been promoted from her original administrative assistant position to this job in the marketing department, Susan wasn't satisfied.

She said, "I don't really like my job—it's boring and uninspiring. How can I get passionate about working on collateral materials and internal communications for a consulting company?"

"What do you like about your job?" I asked.

"A few of the people I work with are nice and we have fun sometimes, when we aren't too stressed or busy. But, overall it's a pretty stuffy and negative place, and the work isn't exciting."

"Susan," I said, "I have a challenge for you. Even though I know you don't love this job, over the next few weeks see if you can pay attention to as much of the good stuff about your job as you can—in a genuine way. Make a list of things you like and appreciate about what you do, the people around you, and the company in general. When we talk next, share that list with me. Okay?"

Susan agreed, somewhat half-heartedly, and made a commitment to focus on the good stuff in her job for the next few weeks as much as she could.

On our next call she said, "It wasn't easy at first to find things that I like and appreciate about my job, but after a few days it started to get easier. I did make a list and actually came up with almost eighty different things— like the flowers in the lobby, the good food in the cafeteria, the problem-solving and time-management skills I've developed over the years as a mom that I get to use almost every day at work, and, most specifically, the people. The more I paid attention to it, the more things I noticed about lots of people around here whom I do like and appreciate."

Over the next few months in our coaching sessions we focused on what Susan was passionate about and what she liked about what she was doing, not so much about all of the "annoying" things about her job. Two interesting things happened as a result of our work together.

First, she started to enjoy her job a lot more—which is what almost always happens when we focus on what we appreciate in a conscious way. And, second, she realized that her real passion was for people. Although the tasks of her job on a daily basis were not the most exciting things in the world to her, Susan began to generate her own sense of passion for her job (and for life in general) by focusing more on the people she was around, and less on her daily activities. By the time we ended our work together, Susan had decided to stay in her current job and was feeling a lot more peaceful and passionate about it.

Ironically, a few months later, she e-mailed me to let me know that she'd gotten a new position within the Human Resources department of her company. She was really excited about this new opportunity and felt like it was an even better fit for her based on her personality and skills.

Here are some things you can do to practice being more passionate and to enhance your own ability to access greater passion on a regular basis:

- Laugh
- Talk about what you're passionate about and ask others what they're passionate about

- Focus on what you appreciate—about yourself, others, and life in general
- Play with children
- Dance (even if you don't think you're good at it)
- Watch the sun rise or set
- Pay attention to people who seem to have a lot of passion and notice what they do and say, and how they interact with life and others
- Walk in nature
- Sing (even if you don't think you're good at it)
- Pay attention to when you feel passionate and notice your thoughts, feelings, body sensations, and more in those moments—so you can re-create them again on purpose
- Listen to music that inspires you

Step Out

One of our greatest sources of authentic power comes from our willingness and ability to act—especially in the face of obstacles and fear. To be authentic in life, we must challenge ourselves to take bold and courageous actions and to go for what we want. Legendary author Ray Bradbury said, "First you jump off the cliff and then you build your wings on the way down."

In the summer of 1998 I was in the midst of a major life transition. I'd blown out my pitching arm a little over a year earlier and had gotten released by the Kansas City Royals that March. I was home in Oakland collecting workers' comp insurance (and not working), recovering from simultaneous elbow and shoulder surgery that I'd had at the start of that summer, reeling from what was sure to be the end of my dream of becoming a Major League baseball player (even after my arm rehab was completed), and trying to figure out what to do with the rest of my life. Throughout that spring and summer, I read numerous self-help books that inspired me—both by what I learned from them personally and also by the idea of being able to write books like that and help people myself. I would wander into bookstores and find myself drawn to the personal development section—both to look for new books to read and also because I had a deep yearning to be involved in that world myself.

Given my age at the time, twenty-four, my lack of experience, and the fact that I had no idea how one would even begin a career as a self-help author, I felt discouraged, scared, and confused. Being an author one day seemed like a pipe dream. And in the weeks and months ahead I knew I'd need to make some important decisions about what to do and what specific steps to take as I ventured out into the "real world" for the very first time.

On July 11, 1998, I had a conversation on the phone with my Uncle Steve that as I look back on it now was a pivotal moment in the course of my life and my work. Steve is married to my mom's younger sister Adele. He's a therapist and an amazing man. He and I have always had a strong connection, even though we've never been able to spend that much time together, since he lives in Texas and I live in California. From the time I was a child, I've always trusted him and been influenced by him deeply. Steve has

been there for me in some of the most important and challenging times in my life.

That day on the phone, I shared with him some of my
deepest fears, dreams, confusion, and desires for my life
and my future. I told him that I thought I wanted to be an
author who could help and inspire people, but that I didn't
know how to do that, where to start, or what I could do in
my life right away that would lead me in that direction.

Steve challenged me and said, "For you to do this
Mike, you're going to have to 'step out' and be bold in your
life. It's not a one-time thing, it's a day-by-day process. The
question to ask yourself today and every day is, 'What am I
willing to do today to step out in life?' "

This question that Steve asked me, while simple to
understand, challenged me to my core—both inspiring
me and scaring me at the same time. I wasn't sure how to
answer that question at the time, but thought about it quite
a bit.

I got a job that fall working for a dot-com company,
but my dream of writing, along with speaking, leading
workshops, and coaching people, stayed with me. Over
those next few years, Steve would send me notes and post-
cards from time to time with just the words "Step Out"
on them. It became a mantra for me in my life, and he
became one of my biggest supporters and sources of inspiration. Even though I knew the job I had selling Internet
advertising was not my "calling," I chose to be grateful for
what I was learning and the money I was making. At the
same time I began to look outside of my current job for

places where I could "step out" toward my deeper passion and dream of helping people. I did this in as many ways as I could—taking workshops; volunteering; reaching out to established authors, speakers, and coaches; talking to people about my goals and dreams; reading books; and much more.

When I got laid off from my dot-com job in the middle of 2000, Steve's question reverberated within me deeply. I knew that the bold thing for me to do at that point, even though I still didn't have a clue about how to go about it, was to "step out" and do what I could to become a speaker, coach, and author. It wasn't easy, and there were many times I wanted to quit—but I kept challenging myself to be bold and to go for it, even when I didn't think I could. It took me six months from the time I got laid off to launch my speaking and coaching business, another two or three years before I was able to establish myself in any significant way, and seven years before I published my first book.

Stepping out is essential in our ability to be bold and live with authenticity in life. We often don't think we're "ready," we may not know exactly what we're supposed to do, and we almost never have a guarantee that things will work out.

Will we get scared? Of course we will. Will we fail? Most likely we will, especially at first. As the cliché says, "no risk, no reward." When we're willing to put ourselves at risk and to go for what we truly want in a bold way, amazing things can happen.

CHECK THIS OUT
Commitment and Boldness

"Until one is committed, there is hesitancy, the chance to draw back, always ineffectiveness. Concerning all acts of initiative and creation, there is one elementary truth the ignorance of which kills countless ideas and splendid plans: that the moment one definitely commits oneself, then providence moves too. All sorts of things occur to help one that would never otherwise have occurred. A whole stream of events issues from the decision, raising in one's favor all manner of unforeseen incidents, meetings and material assistance which no man could have dreamed would have come his way. Whatever you can do or dream you can, begin it. Boldness has genius, power and magic in it. Begin it now."

—Johann Wolfgang von Goethe, 1749–1832

Question to Ask Yourself
What are you willing to do today that means stepping out and going for what you really want in your life in a bold way?

Lean on Others
Another important aspect of being bold is leaning on and getting the support of other people. Being bold, by

its nature, is about us stepping up, stepping out, and taking courageous action in our lives. We often must do this on our own and in many cases in the face of significant fear of criticism, judgment, or ridicule from others, even from those close to us. Although being bold is something we must do alone, it's also essential for us to lean on, get support from, and be both challenged and encouraged by others if we're going to go for what we want in a bold way and live our lives with authenticity.

Do you like to ask others for help? Most people I know and work with, including me, have some issues at times regarding asking for help. We don't want to seem pushy or needy, we don't want to inconvenience someone else, we don't want to count on others and have them let us down.

Do you like helping people? Almost everyone I know really enjoys helping others. It's an honor when someone asks for and receives our help. Of course there are a few exceptions when it can be a little annoying to have people around us who always ask for our help in a selfish way or don't acknowledge us when we do support them, but those are usually the exception and not the rule. By and large, helping and being of service to others is quite fulfilling.

What if we related to our ability to ask for and receive the support of other people as a gift and an opportunity to allow them to help us? Doing so can help us let go of our fear, resistance, and the negative stigma about asking for help that many of us have. In the process, we'll be able to get lots of help and support, which is necessary if we truly want to be bold in life.

Why is leaning on others so important for us in our desire to be bold and authentic? The feedback, support, coaching, encouragement, challenge, accountability, and enthusiasm of other people are all necessary for us to get up and be bold in life—especially when we get scared, confused, or sidetracked in the various ways we do.

Paradoxically, we have to remember that if we make "being bold" all about trying to impress or please people—our friends, family members, spouses, mentors, children, and others—it ends up not being about boldness or authenticity but about performance. However, we've all had many experiences in life when the support, guidance, and accountability of other people forced us outside of our comfort zones and challenged us, in a very positive way, to be bold and to go for what we really wanted.

A great example of this took place with my coaching client Rob. Rob wanted to have more fun, take more risks, and create more success in his life—but didn't know exactly what he wanted to do. After a few sessions together, I suggested that he make a list of things he could do that would scare him, but at the same time would also be great opportunities for him to practice being bold. They could be "big" or "small" things—as long as they would take some real courage on his part to do. After he made his list, his next assignment was to pick something from the list and make it happen.

"Rob, what did you pick?" I asked.

"Singing in public," said Rob.

"Cool. Tell me why this is bold for you," I said.

"Well," said Rob, "when I was a little kid I used to sing all the time—at home, with my mom and sister, and at church in the kid's choir. I even did a few solos in some of our church shows when I was little. Then, when I was about twelve, my voice changed and so did my singing. I've always hated the sound of my singing voice since it changed, and people have made fun of me for years about how bad I sound. Because of this, I just stopped singing. I can't remember the last time I sang in public anywhere. This will be huge for me if I can actually do it—I'm terrified."

Rob wasn't sure when, where, and how he could pull this off. I challenged him to lean on some of his many friends. After procrastinating for a while, Rob asked Mark, his musician friend, if he would help him, coach him a little, and play his guitar while he sang. Mark, of course, said yes. Mark was having a gathering at his house later that week with many of their mutual friends—about twenty people. He suggested to Rob that he sing at the gathering. The stakes were now getting higher for Rob—not only would he be singing in public for the first time in many years, but he'd be doing it in front of people he knew.

The night Rob was supposed to sing at Mark's house, he thought about not showing up. He ended up going, but when he got to the party, he tried to talk his way out of it. Mark and Rob's other friends wouldn't let him off the hook—they knew it was important and that it would be good for him to do it. So, he did. And he was fired up about it when we talked the next time.

Rob said, "I can't believe I actually sang in front of people. I was so scared, my knees were shaking. Even though I don't think I sounded that good, I didn't care. I had fun and so did everyone else. This was such a great exercise for me to do because it taught me that I'm the only one holding me back. I can be bold whenever I choose. And I never would've done it without Mark and my friends challenging and supporting me."

EXERCISE
Step Out and Lean on Others

Step 1

Find someone you trust and talk to them about some of the big things that you want to do, accomplish, or experience in your life (your big goals and dreams). These goals can be very specific, such as starting a business, owning a home in a particular place, writing a book, retiring at a certain age, getting married, and so on. Or they can be more general and experiential, such as being peaceful, relaxed, or fulfilled. Whatever you talk about, be authentic and bold; you want these to be things that are truly important to you—your biggest goals and dreams.

Step 2

For each of these big goals and dreams, think of and talk about specific people you know (or would like to know) whom you could ask for support and lean on to help you make these things happen in your life. You may know someone who's very successful in business whom you could ask for advice or someone else who seems quite relaxed and peaceful whom you could spend time with and learn from.

Step 3

Pick three of the goals and come up with one or more specific actions you could take to either make each of them happen directly or to enlist the support of others whom you could lean on to support you in making them happen. Commit to taking these actions this week and have the person you talk to hold you accountable.

When You Fall Down, Get Back Up

Have you ever seen a small child learn how to walk? It's a remarkable experience. I'd heard about this, but had never witnessed it firsthand until Samantha, our three-year-old, took her first real steps when she was just over a year old. She and I were playing in our family room, and although she'd taken a step or two here and there, and could get around okay while holding onto an adult or a piece of furniture, she hadn't really "walked" yet. That night I was holding her hands and pulling her across the room with me, as she took some steps. I decided to let go to see what would happen. I did and she took a step or two and then fell down, face first, on the soft carpet. She was fine. She looked up at me and although she couldn't speak, she made it very clear that she wanted me to pick her up so she could try again.

I did, and this time when I let go she took about four or five real steps and then fell down. I screamed, "You did it!" started clapping wildly, and yelling for Michelle to come into the room.

Michelle came running in. Samantha and I went to the far end of our family room. I held her hands to steady her, started walking with her across the floor, let go, and then it happened—she really walked—all the way across the room, by herself. When she fell down, Michelle and I were so elated and moved, we both burst into tears and joyous laughter at the same time. Samantha, so proud of herself, began to shriek with excitement and to clap her hands as she was lying there on the floor. And, of course, she wanted to get back up and go again.

We all know how to do this—fall down and get back up. Assuming we know how to walk, which most of us are fortunate enough to be able to do, we went through this specific and miraculous experience ourselves when we were very small. We've also gone through it in a figurative sense many other times as we moved through the ups and downs of life. The question isn't whether or not we'll fall down; the question is will we be bold enough to get back up again? Too often, sadly, we fall down and then decide we can't get back up. Boldness is about having the courage, willingness, and commitment to get back up when we fall down—even if we're scared, embarrassed, or don't think we can.

Resisting, complaining about, or even feeling sorry for ourselves about the "bad" things that happen is totally normal and what we're often encouraged to do by people around us and our culture in general—whether we do it out loud with others or just in our heads. However, these things, while understandable, don't address the real issues—the emotions we're experiencing—or make things better for us. Facing difficulties in our lives can actually be an incredibly rewarding and positive experience for us—if we choose to allow our challenges to be opportunities for growth.

Following is a list of some things we can appreciate when we "fall down" in life. Obstacles, failures, and challenges can

- Give us important feedback about where and who we are
- Provide an opportunity for us to be courageous
- Allow us to wake up and notice all the good things that are happening that we hadn't been paying attention to
- Give us a great opportunity for learning, growth, and improvement
- Allow us to learn to appreciate ourselves, even when things don't turn out exactly as we want them to
- Give us an opportunity to get in touch with, take responsibility for, and express our real emotions in an authentic way
- Challenge us to play bigger, make adjustments, or rethink our approach

By learning to appreciate our challenges and see the opportunities in them, we take our power back from the situations and outcomes of our lives. Our ability to appreciate difficulties, learn from them, and use them to our advantage gives us an important insight into who we really are and how to create success and fulfillment in a conscious, deliberate, and authentic way.

Being bold, going for what we want, and living with authenticity doesn't in any way mean we won't struggle or fall short. In fact, if we aren't failing or facing any challenges at all, it's probably a good indication that we aren't playing all that big in our lives. It's important for us to make peace with the fact that we will fall down many times throughout our journey. However, when we make a commitment to ourselves to get back up, dust ourselves off, be real about how we feel and what happened, and not let it stop us from being who we are and going for what we want—we tap into what true power, boldness, and authenticity are all about.

As Mark Twain reminds us in one of his many famous quotes, "Dance like nobody's watching; love like you've never been hurt. Sing like nobody's listening; live like it's heaven on earth."

PRACTICES

The following are a few powerful practices that you can use in your life to support you in being bold and going for what you want in an effective and authentic way.

1. Ask yourself "the question" every day. "The Question" is, "If today were my last day—what would I do, what would I say, and how would I want to show up in life?" While it may seem a little melodramatic, when we're able to live our lives with a healthy awareness of our own deaths on a daily basis, it alters the way we live and causes us to pay more attention to what's truly important and the people we care about, and, most specifically, it reminds and challenges us to be bold in an authentic way.

2. Write down your goals and dreams and share them with others. When you get in touch with some of your deepest goals and dreams, there are two very important things you can do to help enhance your ability to manifest them in your life. The first thing is to write them down. With my own goals and whenever I work with others, I believe the best way to write goals down is to make sure you put them in specific and positive language in a way that inspires you. It's also a good idea to put them in a format that you're proud of and can access easily. For example, put your goals on nice paper, in frames, and up on the wall somewhere close to you—bedroom, office, and so on. The second thing is to share them with other people whom you respect, trust, and admire. Having your goals seen by others creates a sense of energy, accountability, and support for you and helps make your dreams more possible.

3. Create a dream team. A "dream team" is a group of people that you can lean on, call on, and get support from as you step out and take bold actions. This group can be large or small and can consist of friends, family members, colleagues, mentors, coaches, clients, or anyone else. The idea is to have a group of people to relate to collectively as your "dream team," which means they are resources for you and can support you to be bold, take action, and manifest your dreams. You may want to have a general dream team or one that you set up specifically for a big goal or dream you're working on. Set this up in your own unique way. This isn't about you taking from others in a selfish or needy way, it's about you asking for and receiving the support of other people, and in the process giving others an opportunity to do what most of us love to do—help! It's important to be grateful, gracious, and honoring of anyone and everyone who helps and supports you in a big or small way.

4. Practice taking bold and passionate actions regularly. Come up with a long list of things you could do that would be bold or passionate actions and start taking them on a regular basis. The more you put your attention on being bold and passionate, the more opportunities you'll see in which you can take these kinds of actions. Since this is something that we all can practice in order to improve, it's a good idea to pay attention to and keep track of your bold actions and to challenge yourself to take them on a regular basis. Some simple examples of things you might have on your list are raising your hand in meetings, going on a spontaneous "adventure" with your friends or family, talking to new people you don't know, asking for help, dancing or singing in public, letting people know what you want, or anything else that would be bold or passionate for you.

5. Write a mission and vision statement for your life. Create a personal mission and vision statement for your life, just like organizations do. There are lots of different formulas, formats, and definitions for what these are and how to do them. Don't get too hung up on the process—just do it. Having a mission and a vision for your life that resonates with you and inspires you can support you in being bold and living with authenticity. Your mission is about who you are and how you live on a daily basis. My mission statement is, "I create a world of love and peace by loving myself and reminding others to love themselves." This is written out, printed on gold paper, and hanging in a frame right over my desk. Your vision is about where you want to be and what you want your life to look like and feel like in the future (in other words, where you're headed). It's a future vision, but its intention is to focus you in the present moment on what's most important to you. For your vision, imagine yourself out in the future five, ten, or twenty years from now— write up in detail what your life looks like, how you feel, and what you're experiencing at that time as if it were happening right now. Make it clear and specific but, paradoxically, don't get too hung up on the details, as they will probably change quite a bit.

Being bold is an important aspect of our journey to greater authenticity in our lives. Now that we've gone through the first four principles (Know Yourself, Transform Your Fear, Express Yourself, and Be Bold), we're ready to take a look at the fifth and final principle, which is the foundation for being ourselves in a powerful way: celebrating who we are.

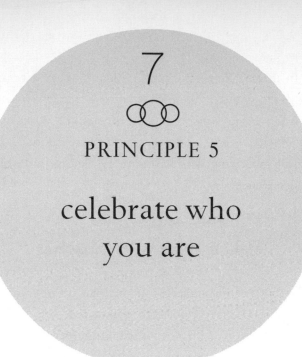

7

PRINCIPLE 5

celebrate who you are

"You, yourself, as much as anybody in the entire universe, deserve your love and affection."

—*Buddha*

We've now arrived at the fifth and final principle, "Celebrate Who You Are." To be our authentic selves, it's essential that we celebrate all of who we are by making peace with and appreciating ourselves completely. Because we spend much of our time and energy focused on what we think is wrong with us, celebrating ourselves doesn't come easy to most of us.

In this chapter we'll take a look at what it means to make peace with and appreciate ourselves and how we can do this in more consistent and meaningful ways in our lives. When we love and appreciate ourselves fully, being ourselves and living with authenticity become a more normal and natural way of being for us.

Making Peace with Ourselves

Making peace with ourselves means that we give ourselves a break and relate to ourselves with a true sense of kindness, compassion, and acceptance. This doesn't mean that we're lazy, irresponsible, or in denial, or that we don't hold ourselves to a high standard—it just means that we get off our own cases and take back our power from the negative voice of that pesky Gremlin who constantly reminds us about all of our "flaws."

We're Okay, Just the Way We Are

When we make peace with ourselves, we remember that we're okay—just as we are. As much as we say we want to do this, we're often worried that if we stopped thinking something was wrong with us, we'd have nothing to motivate us to change, improve, or succeed in life. Because we live in a culture that seems fixated on "more, better, or different," and most of us have an obsession with what we consider to be "bad" about ourselves, it takes a lot of practice to remind ourselves that we're okay just the way we are right now.

A great example of this came in response from my friend Holly to one of my questions as I was doing research for this book. She said,

> I, like most women, pulled out each unwelcomed gray hair at the first sight of them. Rather than literally pull all of my hair out I began dyeing it. After twelve years of dyeing my hair for fear of looking old, my inner voice started screaming at me, "Let your hair go gray." I would shout back, "No, not yet, not ready, I don't want to look old."
>
> "No one will hire me. I'll be less attractive," and on and on I would argue with myself. My deep inner voice was having none of it. It kept insisting that I try it. Finally I relented. I took advantage of a long vacation and decided to let the roots do their thing. I remember my dear friend Jana said she would hold my hand through the process if I felt haggard-looking or old, but that never happened. Instead, something miraculous took place. When I listened to my authentic self, stopped trying to put my finger in the dike of the march of time, and let go of trying to be and look some way I thought I was supposed to, I felt empowered, authentic, and, in fact, more radiant than I'd felt in my youth.
>
> The craziest part is that family, friends, and clients actually like my natural gray hair better. I think I'm able to connect more deeply with people because I'm more real and approachable. Instead of saying sixty is the new forty; I'm saying sixty is the new sixty.

Embracing Our Dark Sides

Another important element of making peace with ourselves and being able to celebrate all of who we are is embracing our "dark sides." This dark side is commonly referred to as our "shadow." The shadow is another important concept that has been expanded upon in psychological, emotional, and spiritual ways by many teachers since Carl Jung introduced it in the mid-twentieth century. All of us have a shadow made up of instincts and emotions suppressed in our unconscious.

According to Jung, "The less the shadow is embodied in the individual's conscious life, the blacker and denser it is." In other words, it's important for us to identify, make peace with, and embrace our shadows, or they can have a significantly debilitating impact on our lives. However, since much of our shadows consist of what we consider to be "negative" or downright "evil," it takes some real courage, commitment, and authenticity to deal with and integrate them into our lives in a positive way.

Because our shadows are unconscious, we often see them first in others before we're able to identify them in ourselves. Whenever we feel ourselves overreacting emotionally to a quality or characteristic in someone else that pushes our buttons, we can be sure that we're seeing a part of our own shadow in that other person. There will often be a repulsive element that resonates deeply within us that we actually identify with. If we don't acknowledge this dark aspect of ourselves, own it, and embrace it within ourselves, whatever quality in them that we can't stand or whatever aspects of ourselves that we have not owned will continue to dominate our lives.

As Debbie Ford, author of *The Dark Side of the Light Chasers* and one of the most insightful modern teachers of shadow work, says, "What you can't own, owns you."

A coach I had a number of years ago named Gwen said to me once, "Mike, you act like a really nice guy on the surface, but underneath that you think you're better than other people, don't you? You can be a real arrogant jerk; even though you pretend to be otherwise."

When she said this, I got defensive and said, "Are you kidding? I'm not like that!" I couldn't believe she would say something like that to me. I was really upset and offended. However, over the next few days I couldn't stop thinking about what Gwen had said.

When we talked the next time, I said to her, "I can't believe you had the nerve to say that to me. I was really mad about it and annoyed with you. But, you know what—you're right! I do think I'm better than other people, although I don't admit it, and underneath my 'nice guy' and humble facade, I can be quite arrogant and sometimes even a real jerk. I realize that I hate these qualities in other people, but I hate them even more within myself. I'm so embarrassed."

Gwen then said to me, "Mike, first of all, I said what I said because I wanted to get your attention—which it sounds like I did. Second of all and more important, there's nothing wrong with you. It's actually good news that you realized you can be an arrogant jerk and that you're starting to see it and own it. Now you can make peace with this 'dark' aspect of yourself and do something about it. Everyone is arrogant sometimes. Accepting it will allow you to claim the 'light side' of arrogance, which can be self-confidence and strength, instead of living your life hiding the fact that sometimes you, too, can be a jerk."

Gwen was right. As Gloria Steinem said, "The truth will set you free. But first, it will piss you off."

Having compassion with ourselves and embracing the dark parts of who we are is liberating. When we can see and accept all of who we are, not just the stuff we think is "good," we have real power and we're able to celebrate ourselves completely. As we discussed in Part One of the book, much of our time and energy is spent trying to cover up, fix, change, or avoid the stuff we think is "bad" about who we are. This takes a lot of energy and causes a lot of stress, suffering, and pain in our lives and for those around us. While there's nothing wrong with wanting to improve certain aspects of ourselves or wanting to change certain qualities we're not proud of, the best way for us to approach this is from a self-accepting and self-loving perspective.

Forgiving Ourselves
Self-forgiveness is also an essential part of making peace with ourselves. I come from a long line of grudge holders on both sides of my family. It has taken a lot of internal work, practice, and forgiveness of myself and others for me to let go of the many grudges I've hung onto in my life. For me and most of us, this is an ongoing process and isn't

always easy. Grudge holding is something many of us have mastered. And the main person we hold grudges against is ourselves. We hang onto issues, failures, and mistakes we make and are often incredibly hard on ourselves about them. We give our power over to our Gremlins and let negativity and self-criticism get the best of us.

Self-forgiveness is not some flowery way of letting ourselves off the hook by avoiding accountability and personal responsibility. True self-forgiveness, in fact, is just the opposite. When we face our weaknesses, failures, or mistakes directly, take responsibility for them, make amends if necessary, and ultimately forgive ourselves, we're able to learn, grow, and move on from the biggest shortcomings, setbacks, and difficulties we face in life.

In regard to self-forgiveness, my friend Jonathan said,

When I accepted my sexuality, it was the single scariest and most liberating thing I'd ever done. I was married to a woman at the time, a "pillar in the community," and I had a budding and promising career. I knew I would be ostracized by many and that it would rattle the world of my family. Yet I couldn't deny who I was any longer.

I had to forgive myself for lying about who I really was for so long, for hurting and betraying the trust of many people who loved me, and for being too scared to deal with this for almost thirty years.

In the end, after all of the shuddering, the pain that was caused, and eventual acceptance and forgiveness, all is finally right and congruent in my world. I only began any kind of authenticity and peace in my life when I "came out."

What can you forgive yourself for and let go of right now?

CHECK THIS OUT
The Many Benefits of Forgiveness

According to researchers at the world-famous Mayo Clinic, scientific evidence tells us that holding onto grudges and bitterness results in long-term health problems. Forgiveness, on the other hand, offers numerous benefits, including

- Lower blood pressure
- Stress reduction
- Less hostility
- Better anger-management skills
- Lower heart rate
- Lower risk of alcohol or substance abuse
- Fewer depression symptoms
- Fewer anxiety symptoms
- Reduction in chronic pain
- More friendships
- Healthier relationships
- Greater religious or spiritual well-being
- Improved psychological well-being

Appreciating Ourselves

When we love, value, and acknowledge ourselves both for what we do and, more important, for who we are, we appreciate ourselves.

Here's a list of some simple examples of self-appreciation:

- Celebrating our success
- Speaking about ourselves in a positive way
- Accepting compliments with gratitude and ease
- Forgiving ourselves and our mistakes
- Taking care of ourselves—physically, emotionally, mentally, and spiritually

Genuine self-appreciation is often way below the waterline for us and isn't something that's all that socially acceptable. This takes courage and vulnerability on our part. We're expected to be self-deprecating and modest, and to not think too highly of ourselves—which is ultimately ridiculous, because at the same time we're supposed to believe in ourselves, have confidence, and trust ourselves in life. When we have the courage to appreciate ourselves fully, it's one of the most generous and authentic things we can do to honor, support, and empower who we are in a genuine way.

CHECK THIS OUT
Great Quote

According to author and psychotherapist Bobbe Sommer, Ph.D., "Having a low opinion of yourself is not 'modesty,' it's self-destruction. Holding your uniqueness in high regard is not 'egotism,' it's a necessary precondition to happiness and success."

We Are Each Unique

There is and only ever will be one of each of us. And while we know this and have been told this many times in our lives, even by some of the same parents, teachers, ministers, friends, coaches, family members, and others whom we learned to be inauthentic from—they were right when they said this. Sadly, we either forgot, chose not to pay attention, or didn't believe them in the first place. We end up spending most of our lives trying to be like others, wishing we were some way that we're not or can't be, or devaluing ourselves in a way that doesn't honor or acknowledge our uniqueness.

In June of 2008, the world of media and politics lost an icon when Tim Russert, host of NBC's *Meet the Press*, passed away suddenly of a heart attack. The outpouring of grief and appreciation for Russert's death was quite remarkable and moving. Michelle and I were big fans of Tim Russert, and I found myself deeply saddened by his death and inspired by his life, even though I only knew him through television. As I watched many of the interviews, retrospective shows, and memorials to him in the days following his passing, I was struck by two specific things about Tim Russert. First of all, he was himself authentically—which is what had led so many people to trust him, appreciate him, and respect him. Second, he was unique.

His version of being unique wasn't that he was flashy, polished, or overtly "different," it was that he was true to himself, his values, and what seemed important to him.

A small-town kid from Buffalo, New York, who loved football, his family, and his country, Tim Russert didn't try to be anything he wasn't, and it came across in his work on TV, in his books, and, from what so many people who knew him said after he passed away, in his personal relationships. In his life and his death, Tim Russert was and is a great reminder to us of the power of being ourselves and embracing our unique gifts and talents in an authentic way.

Honoring Ourselves

When we honor ourselves, we appreciate and celebrate who we are in an authentic way. Honoring ourselves means that we respect and take care of ourselves. We often get busy, being focused on taking care of everyone else, and we worry that if we take the time to care for ourselves, people would think we're selfish, narcissistic, or self-absorbed. The opposite is true.

I was talking to my friend Leslie about this phenomenon, and she shared an insightful and vulnerable perspective with me. Leslie said,

> Mike, as my girls got older and became teenagers and then young women, I found myself getting both concerned and frustrated that neither of them seemed to be doing a very good job of taking care of or honoring themselves—physically, emotionally, or professionally. This caused a

good amount of stress for me and created some conflict in my relationships with both of them. As I looked at this a bit deeper and thought back to how I raised them, I realized that when they were growing up I did everything I could to take care of them and their father—giving of myself in every possible way while doing my best to keep the family together, make money, and everything else I had going on. However, what I never showed my girls was an example of a grown woman honoring or taking care of herself. I then could understand and have compassion for why they were each struggling to do just that given the model they had from me.

Here are some things you can do to honor yourself more effectively:

- Use positive and loving words when talking about yourself
- Take care of yourself and your needs first, then take care of those around you
- Ask for what you want specifically
- Say "no" when you need to
- Listen to your gut or intuition
- Stand up for what's important to you
- Rest
- Trust yourself
- Request and accept support from others
- Do things that you enjoy
- Have fun
- When someone compliments you, just say "thank you" and let it in

Owning Our Greatness

The great Buckminster Fuller said, "I am convinced all of humanity is born with more gifts than we know. Most are born geniuses and just get de-geniused rapidly."

We often sell out on our true greatness—giving in to our fears, doubts, and insecurities or simply letting our Gremlins take over and convince us that we "can't." Owning our "greatness" is not about competing with people or comparing ourselves to others. It has nothing to do with anyone else and has everything to do with who we are, the natural talents we have, and our ability to allow our own lights to shine. This is one of the biggest and most important challenges of our lives. We spend and waste so much time worrying about what other people think, trying to fit in, or hoping we don't mess things up, and in the process we miss out on who we really are, why we're here, and the brilliance and beauty within us that we have to share with others and with the world around us.

Think of the times in your life when you were able to get out of your own way and let your true greatness come through. For most of us, these are the most exhilarating, exciting, and rewarding moments in life—even if they're scary or painful initially. Here are some things you can do to practice owning your greatness more often:

- Acknowledge and appreciate yourself all the time
- Take risks and "go for it" whenever you have the chance
- Stop apologizing for yourself
- Celebrate your failures as much or more than your successes

- Focus on your strengths
- Don't take yourself too seriously
- Surround yourself with exceptional, compassionate, and supportive people
- Be grateful

Whatever we admire in others is also true at some deep level about ourselves as well. This is the opposite of our dark sides or shadows that we discussed earlier. Our "light shadows" are made up of many of the repressed gifts, talents, and positive qualities within us that we have forgotten about or been led to believe we don't possess. When we see things in other people that we are inspired by, drawn to, or excited about—those are aspects of our light shadows.

This doesn't mean that we can perform the same functions or have the same specific talents that other people do, but it does mean that the below-the-line qualities within others that allow them to manifest success and fulfillment also exist within us, as they do in every other human being. This concept isn't usually easy for us to understand and practice because we've been trained from the time we were children to compete with others, to compare ourselves to them, and to live in the world of scarcity in which we believe there's only so much to go around and we're all separate from one another. When we begin to let go of these and other negative, limiting, and erroneous notions that have us play small in life, we can step into our power and our greatness by owning who we really are.

In response to one of my questions about being authentic and going for it in life, my friend Scott said,

I was the producer and writer for a documentary I had begged to be on. It was considered out of my league, but finally I was given the green light. It was a sports documentary on a cycling race, like the Tour de France, to be aired in primetime. I chose to approach the documentary as a story that started with the end result. It was a little unconventional for a sports documentary at the time—but it felt right to me, I knew we could pull it off, and believed in my gut it was going to be a big success.

The network program executives were in town, and the TV station wanted me to show them what I had so far. There was palpable silence after they viewed it. I could tell they didn't like what they saw. The station programming executive said it didn't work and that I needed to come at it from a more conventional route. He said I had to scrap it and start over.

When I got back into the editing booth with my editor, I ranted and raved and made a decision that changed my career. I told my editor he could opt out of working on it, but I was not going to change it. I knew it worked for a primetime audience that understood nothing of bicycling. My editor didn't abandon me. We finished it after having been awake about a hundred hours. It aired as we delivered it and won several awards including the Emmy Award for best sports program and best videography.

Self-Love—The Ultimate Goal

The ultimate goal of being ourselves in an authentic way is to love ourselves completely. If we truly love ourselves, most of what we worry about and even much of what we strive for in life becomes meaningless. We may still have some worries, and we'll definitely continue to have goals, dreams, and desires. However, from a place of true self-appreciation and self love, the fear behind our worries and the motivation for our goals dramatically changes from something we have to avoid or produce in order to get love to something we genuinely are concerned about or something we really want to accomplish.

On the flip side, if we don't love ourselves, nothing much really matters. No matter what we conquer, create, or experience we're never able to appreciate it, ourselves, or to be fulfilled in the process, because we're constantly striving to be loved and validated.

Self-love is what we're all searching for. Sadly, we spend most of our lives thinking that someone or something else can give us what only we can give ourselves. To be fulfilled in life, we have to find the love within us and give it to ourselves. No other person, amount of money, material possession, or accomplishment can do it. It's up to us. We have an opportunity to celebrate ourselves for any reason and at any time.

Loving myself is something that I both strive for and struggle with in my own day-to-day life. I spend a good amount of my time and energy attempting to love myself, sometimes more effectively than at other times. In my best

moments, I know the amazing peace, gratitude, and fulfillment that come from self-love. I love how it feels, how the
world looks, how I treat myself, and how I relate to others. When I love myself, I'm available to give to myself and
to others in a free, open, generous, and authentic way—
which, for me, is the most important thing in life. In my
lowest moments, I know the pain and suffering of not loving myself and I see what impact this has on my work, my
relationships, my family, and my life.

I wish I could say I had the "magic formula" for how
we can love ourselves unconditionally. I don't, and I'm not
sure anyone does. It's a personal journey we all must take
in our lives, and it happens in the moment-by-moment
experiences of our lives. When we're willing to acknowledge both the challenge and the power of self-love and
remember that loving ourselves is the ultimate goal, we're
reminded of the necessity to do everything we can to celebrate all of who we are in an authentic way.

Imagine what your life would be like if you fully and
completely loved yourself? Imagine what the world would
look like if we all loved ourselves?

EXERCISE
Write a Love Letter to Yourself

This is a powerful exercise that I sometimes do with my
clients and in my workshops. To do this effectively, you'll
have to lower your waterline, get real, and be willing to

express love and appreciation for yourself in a vulnerable, bold, and authentic way.

Step 1

Take some time to think about and feel the love you have for yourself. What do you appreciate about yourself? What are you proud of? What can you acknowledge yourself for? Imagine you're writing a love letter to someone you love deeply. In this case, that person is you. This may take some time. You may have to confront your Gremlin, your fear, or any self-criticism, judgment, or cynicism you have about yourself or toward expressing love for yourself in this way.

Step 2

Take out a piece of paper and write a heartfelt love letter to yourself—expressing your love, affection, appreciation, and gratitude for yourself. Be as generous and bold as you can in your expression of love for yourself. Thank yourself for all that you do, what you've accomplished, the risks you've taken, and even the failures, setbacks, and mistakes you've made. Most important, thank, appreciate, and love yourself for the person that you are—behind every success, failure, action, emotion, and everything else in your life is the real you . . . express your love for that person as deeply as you can.

Step 3

Seal the letter, put your own name and address on it, along with a stamp, and give it to someone you trust. Let this other person know that this is a sacred letter that you've

written to yourself and that you'd like them to mail it to
you sometime in the next year—whenever they choose to.
They can mail it the next day, the following week, three
months from then, or at the end of the year. Feel free to
tell them as much or as little about the content of the letter or the details of the exercise, it's up to you. If you let
them know all about it, they might even be inspired to do
their own love letter to themselves and then give it to
you to mail to them. This can be a fun way to get support
and to support another. Either way, give the letter away, ask
for it to be mailed to you, and trust that it will show up in
your mailbox at the perfect time . . . it always does!

PRACTICES

The following are a few practices that you can use in your
life to support you in appreciating and celebrating yourself
in a powerful and authentic way.

1. Work with your shadow. In your personal work with
yourself, in your relationships with others, in your work
with your coach or counselor, and in the workshops you
take—pay attention to your shadow, and begin or continue
to make peace with and embrace it. The best book I've read
on this subject is Debbie Ford's *The Dark Side of the Light Chasers*,
which I mentioned previously in this chapter. Debbie also

offers a three-day intensive workshop called "The Shadow Process," which Michelle and I have done. I highly recommend it. Whatever method you choose, make sure that part of your growth journey includes some shadow work—it's essential, in general and especially as it relates to you being yourself, celebrating all of who you are, and living with authenticity.

2. Make time to celebrate. When something happens that's important to you—big or small—make the effort to celebrate it, acknowledge it, and make a big deal about it. It could be a birthday; an anniversary; a new job; a big risk you've taken; or even the regular daily activities, events, and interactions of your life. For example, take time each night at dinner to celebrate yourself, your life, the people around you, and your day. Or each year at New Year's celebrate the year and all of its ups and downs.

3. Practice positive self-affirmations. Affirmations are powerful. There is now scientific proof that our thoughts, feelings, and words have a much bigger impact on our health, relationships, and the outcomes of our lives than we previously believed. The most important conversation we have all day every day is the conversation with ourselves, about ourselves. Since our Gremlins often run our internal dialogue, most of our thoughts and "self-talk" are quite negative. One of the best ways to break this cycle and practice appreciating and celebrating ourselves is to practice positive self-affirmations—in our minds and out loud on a regular basis. The key to any affirmation is *feeling* it while we're thinking it or saying it. Sometimes at first it may feel a little like you're "faking it," but after you say and think a particular affirmation regularly, you can start to feel it more deeply and begin to believe it. Our thoughts and words don't just describe, they create. One of the best ways to do your affirmations is to speak them directly to yourself in the mirror.

4. Create a regular self-appreciation practice. Taking time to appreciate yourself on a regular basis is one of the best things you can do. In addition to or in conjunction with your affirmations, you can create a simple self-appreciation practice for yourself on a regular basis, ideally daily, which can vary as much as you'd like. Write in your journal a few things each day that you appreciate about yourself. In your meditations or prayers, focus on some things you appreciate about yourself. As you're laying in bed in the morning before you get up or as you drift off to sleep at night, think about some things you're proud of and appreciate about yourself. Talk to a friend, family member, significant other, or anyone you trust and share back and forth about something you each appreciate about yourselves. It's not as important what you do specifically, but that you take some time on a daily basis, like bathing, to appreciate who you are and to do it in a genuine way.

The five principles we've discussed in the previous five chapters, Principle 1, Know Yourself; Principle 2, Transform

Your Fear; Principle 3, Express Yourself; Principle 4, Be Bold; and Principle 5, Celebrate Who You Are, are each essential aspects of being ourselves and living a life of authenticity. Living these principles and utilizing the suggested practices will have you become more real and more of who you truly are in your work, your relationships, and your life.

Now that we've looked at both the reasons why being ourselves can be difficult (the external message and internal beliefs that stop us) and how we can utilize the power of authenticity in our lives (the five principles), we turn our attention to the final, critical piece of this process: action. It's not usually what we know but what we do and practice that really makes a difference in our lives. The next and final chapter focuses on how to put all of this information and inspiration into action in your life in a real way.

part three

authenticity in action

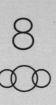

8

living your
authentic life

"Go confidently in the direction of your dreams. Live the
life you have imagined."

—Henry David Thoreau

This final chapter is about taking what we've discussed
in this book and putting it into action in your life in
a meaningful way. I'll recap the most essential points
and talk about the importance of action, accountability, and
support. Immediately following this final chapter is a section of resources (books, audios, videos, and workshops)
that you can utilize to further your personal growth and
development—as they relate to authenticity, and in general.

The goal of this last chapter is to wrap things up and give you a launching pad for living your life in a more authentic and fulfilling way.

What *Was* This Book About, Anyway?

Be Yourself, Everyone Else Is Already Taken was set up in two distinctive parts. Part One addressed why it can be difficult for us to be authentic in our work, in our relationships, and in our lives. Part Two focused on the five principles of authenticity—how to practice being more real in your day-to-day life.

Part One: Why It Can Be Hard to Be Authentic

Being authentic can be challenging for most of us for a variety of reasons. Chapter One looked at some of the external and cultural factors, while Chapter Two looked at the more personal reasons we often struggle to be who we truly are in life. The key points of Part One were

- Most of us aren't taught by our families or the culture in which we live to be ourselves and be authentic.
- We get messages from a variety of sources (family, school, organized religion, politics, media, and more)

that often influence us and have us think we can't be who we really are.

- We've each created a "persona"—an inauthentic way to make it in life that covers many real aspects of ourselves and is all about getting by, looking good, and not having people find out the "bad" stuff about us that we don't want them to know.

- Self-criticism has us focus much of our time and attention on what we think is wrong with us and what we assume needs to be fixed—thus leading us to think that who we are is not good enough.

- Fear is the biggest barrier to our authenticity—we're often scared to be who we are, say what we really mean, and express ourselves authentically because we fear the judgments or rejection of others.

It's important for us to acknowledge, tell the truth about, and take responsibility for these external and internal factors of our lives and personalities that have made it difficult and scary for us to live in a way that is authentic. It's also essential that we do this with a great deal of compassion and understanding. There's nothing wrong with us—being authentic is challenging for almost everyone. Part One was designed to delve deeply into the cultural and personal factors that get in the way of our living an authentic life. By confronting these things directly, owning them, and making peace with them, we're able to move beyond what normally stops us from being who we truly are to live a life of authenticity.

Part Two: The Five Principles of Authenticity

The five principles of authenticity that made up Part Two were designed to empower you with new ideas, perspectives, and tips for greater authenticity and fulfillment in your work, your relationships, and your life.

Principle 1: Know Yourself

Knowing ourselves is the first step to being ourselves in an authentic way. It takes courage to really look within and become aware of who we truly are at the deepest level. Our commitment to personal growth, to discovering more of who we are, and to allowing the support, honest feedback, and guidance of others is essential in our ability to know ourselves and thus be authentic.

Principle 2: Transform Your Fear

We all get scared in life, especially when we live, speak, and act in an authentic way. There's nothing wrong with us for feeling fear; it's one of the most basic and common human emotions. Our resistance to and denial of our fear are the real problems. When we're able to admit, own, feel, and express our fear, we have the ability to transform it and utilize its power in a positive way. Taking action in the face of our fear is courageous and empowering. Being able to feel our fear and at the same time not allow it to stop us is essential in our commitment to live with authenticity.

Principle 3: Express Yourself

Expressing ourselves fully is one of the most important aspects of being authentic. When we have the courage to speak our truth, deal with conflicts directly, and express our emotions completely, we empower ourselves to be who we really are with others and in life in general. Being vulnerable and real, which on the surface are often seen as "weak," in actuality are what give us access to authenticity, freedom, and power in our lives, our work, and our relationships.

Principle 4: Be Bold

Being bold is about living, speaking, and acting with courage and authenticity. It takes boldness to be true to ourselves and live an authentic life. Things we can do to be bold in our lives are be true to ourselves, live with passion, step out, lean on others, and when we fall down, get back up. When we remember and practice these important elements of boldness with courage, we're able to be who we truly are in a bold and authentic way.

Principle 5: Celebrate Who You Are

Celebrating who we are, completely, is the most important element to truly being ourselves. This is not about being arrogant or perfect, or having everything handled in life—it's about accepting, acknowledging, and owning all of who we are, both our light sides and our dark sides, and choosing to celebrate ourselves. There is and only ever will be one of each of us. It's our challenge in life to love ourselves in a genuine way if we want to live with a true sense of authenticity, fulfillment, and confidence. Being who we really are is all about celebrating ourselves.

⚬⚬⚬

These five principles of authenticity are powerful concepts that, with commitment, awareness, and courage, can be incorporated into your life on a regular basis. Each principle builds on the one before it, leading you through a process that starts with knowing yourself, then looks at confronting and transforming your fear, moves on to expressing yourself fully, continues with you being bold, and concludes with the most essential aspect of all: celebrating and loving who you are.

Authenticity in Action

As you finish reading this book, there are two essential questions to ask yourself:

1. How does all of this information relate to me and my life?
2. What can I do to integrate more authenticity into my relationships, my work, and my life on a daily basis?

The Power of Action

Reading a book is a wonderful thing to do—it can expand our minds, give us new ideas and insights, and help us tap into new thoughts and feelings that are essential for our growth. However, it's in the application of these new ideas and techniques that our lives can transform and where growth really happens.

We often know exactly what we need to do to make positive changes in our lives—to get in touch with who we are; to know our truth; and to see, feel, and recognize what's authentic for us. However, it's a totally different thing to act on this, speak it out loud, and make a commitment to live in a way that is true to ourselves—which is what's necessary if we're going to expand our ability to be ourselves and be authentic.

Putting Authenticity into Action in Your Life

Throughout this book there have been many suggestions of possible actions and practices. You've done exercises, learned a powerful technique for transforming your fear, were challenged to "lower your waterline" by letting others know more of who you really are, and much more. You also were given a list of practices at the end of each of the five principles of authenticity that were designed to have you put the ideas of each principle into action in your life. Just through reading this book, you've already taken a number of actions that can bring more authenticity and fulfillment into your work, relationships, and life.

The key is to take some of the actions and ideas from this book, or others that you've come up with, and to put them into practice in your life on a regular basis. Creating regular practices will allow you to expand and improve your ability to know yourself; feel and transform your fear and other emotions; speak your truth; be bold; and, most important, celebrate who you are!

It's a great idea to go back through the book and your notes and pick out a handful of the exercises, techniques, or practices that were mentioned or that you completed. You can also think of other actions or practices that you can take, related to authenticity—ones that you know will work for your unique personality and style. When you put these practices into action in a committed and consistent way in your life, it can literally transform! What specific practices will you now put into action in your life as a result of reading this book and doing these exercises?

Accountability and Support

Accountability and support can be magical, and they're both essential for our growth, success, and fulfillment in life. Whenever I coach someone, my job is to hold them accountable and to support them so they take positive actions toward their most important goals and dreams. By simply making regular commitments about what you'll do and what you want to manifest in your life, you can produce breakthrough results and expand yourself in ways you didn't think you could.

In my own life, I've had some amazing coaches, mentors, and success partners who've all played a vital role in my own success and growth. They've supported me and pushed me by holding me accountable, challenging me, and acknowledging me. Without accountability and support, many of our good ideas and intentions stay as just ideas and intentions. With accountability and support, we're able to put them into action, and we don't have to do it all by ourselves. Because being authentic can be scary, difficult, and challenging at times, it's so important that we have other people we can lean on and get support from, and who can push us when we need pushing, love us when we need loving, and walk with us when we need partnership and encouragement.

Fundamentally, being ourselves in life and living with authenticity comes down to choice, commitment, and courage. What kind of life do you want? How do you want to show up, relate to others, and engage in the journey of your life? Given that you have read all the way through to this point, I assume that having real relationships, being who you are in your work, speaking your truth, going for what you truly want, and living an authentic life are all things that are very important to you.

A Final Word of Acknowledgment for You

As we come to the end of this journey, I want you to know how grateful and honored I am that you trusted me to lead you through this very personal and important process. I hope it has been rewarding for you, and I appreciate your willingness to look deep within yourself. I acknowledge you for your commitment to truth, growth, and realness— in your life and in general.

I wish you all the best on your continued path of growth, discovery, and authenticity. Please let me know how things are going—feel free to contact me through my Website, listed below. And remember, be yourself, everyone else is already taken!

With appreciation,

Mike Robbins

www.mike-robbins.com

resources

ere you will find a list of resources (books, work-shops, audios, videos, Websites, organizations, and so on) that I believe in and recommend strongly. Each of them will support and empower you on your path of personal growth and authenticity. Some of these resources are specifically focused on authenticity and being yourself, whereas some are more generally focused on personal and spiritual development. Either way, check any or all of them out.

Books

Some of these books were referenced specifically through-out the book. All of these titles are great and will enhance your growth, success, and fulfillment.

Actualizations: You Don't Have to Rehearse to Be Yourself, by Stewart Emery
An Hour to Live, An Hour to Love, by Richard and Kris Carlson
The Astonishing Power of Emotions, by Esther and Jerry Hicks
Be Heard Now, by Lee Glickstein
Be Here Now, by Ram Dass
Be Yourself, by John Buffini
Conversations with God, by Neale Donald Walsch
The Dark Side of the Light Chasers, by Debbie Ford
Embracing Fear, by Thom Rutledge

The Energy Addict, by Jon Gordon

Excuse Me Your Life Is Waiting, by Lynn Grabhorn

Extreme Success, by Rich Fettke

Fearproof Your Life, by Joe Bailey

Feel the Fear and Do It Anyway, by Susan Jeffers

The Five Dysfunctions of a Team, by Patrick Lencioni

Five Wishes, by Gay Hendricks

Focus on the Good Stuff, by Mike Robbins

Forget Perfect, by Lisa Earle McLeod

Forgive for Good, by Fred Luskin

The Four Agreements, by Don Miguel Ruiz

The Four-Hour Workweek, by Timothy Ferriss

Getting Real, by Susan Campbell

The Last Lecture, by Randy Pausch and Jeffrey Zaslow

Love Your Body, by Louise Hay

Loving What Is, by Byron Katie

Make Your Creative Dreams Real, by SARK

Many Lives, Many Masters, by Brian Weiss

A New Earth, by Eckhart Tolle

Nonviolent Communication, by Marshall Rosenberg

Now Discover Your Strengths, by Marcus Buckingham and Donald
    Clifton

The Passion Test, by Janet Bray Attwood and Chris Attwood

The Power of Now, by Eckhart Tolle

Pulling Your Own Strings, by Wayne Dyer

Radical Honesty, by Brad Blanton

A Return to Love, by Marianne Williamson

Rich Dad, Poor Dad, by Robert Kiyosaki

Sacred Commerce, by Matthew and Terces Engelhart

Sacred Journey, by Lazaris

The Secret, by Rhonda Byrne

Secrets of the Millionaire Mind, by T. Harv Eker

The Seven Spiritual Laws of Success, by Deepak Chopra
Shut Up, Stop Whining, and Get a Life, by Larry Winget
The Soul of Money, by Lynne Twist
Spiritual Liberation, by Michael Bernard Beckwith
The Success Principles, by Jack Canfield
Unlimited Power, by Anthony Robbins
Way of the Peaceful Warrior, by Dan Millman
The Way of the Superior Man, by David Deida
What About the Big Stuff? by Richard Carlson
When Prayers Aren't Answered, by John Welshons
Will You Still Love Me If I Don't Win? by Christopher Andersonn
Working with Your Shadow, by Lazaris
You Can Heal Your Life, by Louise Hay

Workshops

The Abounding River www.cafegratitude.com/workshops
The Arete Experience www.aretecenter.com
Celebrating Men, Satisfying Women (for women only)
        www.understandmen.com
The Landmark Forum www.landmarkforum.com
The LoveLaunch Weekend www.lifelaunchtraining.com
The Millionaire Mind Intensive www.millionairemind.com
The New Warrior Training Adventure (for men only) www
        .mkp.org
The Next Step www.challengeday.org
The Shadow Process www.integrativecoaching.com
Unleash the Power Within www.tonyrobbins.com

Other Resources

"Appreciation in Action" (free e-mail newsletter) www
        .mike-robbins.com

Agape International Spiritual Center (Extraordinary New
    Thought Spiritual Center) www.agapelive.com
Be Yourself, Everyone Else Is Already Taken (audio), by Mike
    Robbins www.mike-robbins.com
Café Gratitude (Inspiring raw food café)
    www.cafegratitude.com
Challenge Day (Amazing youth peace organization)
    www.challengeday.org
Focus on the Good Stuff (audio), by Mike Robbins
    www.mike-robbins.com
Hay House (Personal growth events, products, radio shows,
    and more) www.hayhouse.com
Life Visioning (audio program), by Michael Bernard Beck-
    with www.agapelive.com/bookstore
The Moses Code (video) www.themosescode.com
Nonviolent Communications (Incredible conflict resolution
    work) www.cnvc.org
The Peace Alliance (International peace organization)
    www.thepeacealliance.org
The Power of Appreciation (audio), by Mike Robbins
    www.mike-robbins.com
The Secret (video) www.thesecret.tv
SelfGrowth.com (Personal development Website)
    www.selfgrowth.com
What the Bleep Do We Know!? (video)
    www.whatthebleep.com
Winning Strategies (box set of audios and videos) www
    .mike-robbins.com
"The Work" by Byron Katie www.thework.com
You Can Heal Your Life (video) www.hayhouse.com

about the author

M ike Robbins delivers motivational keynote addresses, personal development workshops, and coaching programs for individuals, groups, and organizations. He works with corporations, government agencies, associations, nonprofits, and people from all walks of life. Through his speaking, coaching, and consulting business, Mike empowers people to be successful and authentic, to create meaningful relationships, and to appreciate themselves and those around them.

Prior to becoming an author, speaker, and coach, Mike was drafted by the New York Yankees out of high school but chose instead to play baseball at Stanford University, where he pitched in the College World Series. He then played professionally in the Kansas City Royals organization, before an injury cut his baseball career short. After baseball, he worked in advertising sales and business development for two Internet startup companies.

Mike is the author of *Focus on the Good Stuff: The Power of Appreciation* and a contributing author to *Chicken Soup for the Single Parent's Soul*. He's been featured on *ABC News* and the *Oprah and Friends* radio network, as well as in *Forbes*, *Ladies' Home Journal*, the *Washington Post*, and many other publications. His organizational clients include Chevron, Wells Fargo Bank, the U.S. Department of Labor, the Arizona Diamondbacks, AT&T, and many others.

Mike, his wife, Michelle, and their two young daughters, Samantha and Annarose, live in the San Francisco Bay Area. For more information on Mike's work, his keynotes, seminars, and other services, visit www.mike-robbins.com.